D1093955

The Heel of Elohim

Hyatt Howe Waggoner

is a graduate of Middlebury College
and the University of Chicago, and
holds the Ph.D. degree from Ohio
State University. Currently associ-
ate professor of English in the University of Kansas City, he is well
known for his many articles that
have appeared in the literary journals on subjects in American literature, especially in the field of
criticism.

Of all that amplitude that time explores,
A needle in the sight, suspended north,—
Yielding by inference and discard, faith
And true appointment from the hidden shoal:
This disposition that thy night relates
From Moon to Saturn in one sapphire wheel:
The orbic wake of thy once swirling feet,
Elohim, still I hear thy sounding heel!

—HART CRANE *in* The Bridge

The Heel
of Elohim

SCIENCE AND VALUES IN
MODERN AMERICAN POETRY

By Hyatt Howe Waggoner

NORMAN : UNIVERSITY OF OKLAHOMA PRESS

For Louise, Veronica, *and* Jane

WHO DAILY REMIND ME THAT VALUES ARE
IMBEDDED IN THE NATURE OF THINGS

Prefatory Note: Origins, Assumptions, Intentions

Science, poetry, religion—these three between them include a very large share of those values that distinguish human life from animal existence. The Good, the True, and the Beautiful, technique and end, efficient and final causes, all are herein comprehended. Yet we tend to feel today that they are yoked together with violence if at all. A quarter of a century ago we thought we knew what the proper relationship between them was: science was not only the proper study but the true salvation of mankind; poetry was a threatened, perhaps a dying relic of unscientific ages; religion, for the well-informed, was safely dead. Essays were written on the future of poetry in which it was always asked, Can poetry survive in an age of science? Professor I. A. Richards, the founder, as many think, of the new criticism, spoke for his time when in *Science and Poetry* he predicted that poetry might have a future if it became "pure," by which he meant if it abandoned to science all its claims to dealing in knowledge and truth and recognized that the only statements proper to it are "pseudo-statements," the only language "emotive."

Although poetry has become notably more complex and obscure, and even, in a sense, pure, if by "pure" we mean not explicitly didactic, yet the best modern poets have not written very much pure poetry in the sense intended by Mr. Richards, and poetry has survived. Mr. Richards' brash and somewhat ridiculous little book (he has written many others for which one must have considerable respect) has been rather generally forgotten and can be read today only as a revelation of the follies generated by the positivistic materialism of the early twentieth century. Yet some of the issues it raises are still with us, as witness the intensive study of the relations of the language of poetry and the language of science that has been so prominent an aspect of the critical and philosophical achievement of the last quarter-century. If as critics we no longer wonder whether poetry will survive, as philosophers we are concerned with "the place of value in a world of fact" and as critics with a proper statement of the way in which it can be said that poetry conveys knowledge.

The rediscovery of religious values by many intellectuals in the past few years has, like the progress of criticism beyond the point reached by the early works of Mr. Richards and like the continued survival, the positive flourishing, of a type of poetry for which Mr. Richards could see no future, had its effect in altering the questions we ask about the relations of poetry and science. Though religion may be only feebly operative in our society, it is at least no longer clear that it is safely dead. Whether that fact means the hope of a saving age of faith or the danger of a new age of barbarism depends on one's point of view; but it is a fact. Positivists are increasingly alarmed at "the new failure of nerve," those who see religion as something more than blended superstition and ignorance are somewhat inclined to be hopeful; both agree that something is happening today that throws new light on religious, and so on all, values.

Critics analyze poetry in terms of myth and do not mean that poetry deals with the unreal or the superstitious. Poets and novelists follow Mr. Eliot into the church. Critics discover that fictional naturalism has run its course and that at best it was severely limited in the quantity and quality of reality it could reveal. The same kinds of young people who in the twenties were followers of Mencken are now devoted to Charles Williams. Scientists argue that science itself must become "humanistic" and philosophical. Jung's psychology, capable of a religious interpretation, is absorbed into literary criticism. Books like Lecomte du Nouy's *Human Destiny* start heated debates in academic circles. Arnold Toynbee, who is thought by bright young historians with neo-Marxist leanings to have spoiled his history by taking his cue from myth and some of his assumptions from Christianity, is studied as seriously as Spengler was twenty-five years ago, and by the same sort of people. These are straws in the wind. Poetry has survived, and religion is not safely dead. All of which means that an examination of the relations of science and poetry must be undertaken today in very different terms from those of Mr. Richards.

Just what those terms are in this volume I think I should try to state immediately. For scientific "objectivity"—which in literary scholarship and particularly in criticism seems to me an ideal either impossible to attain or attainable only at the price of triviality—is particularly impossible of attainment in such a study as this. But simple honesty requires that one state one's assumptions so far as he is conscious of them; for the assumptions we start with help to shape the questions we ask, and the questions we ask set the limits of the kinds of answers we arrive at—which is to acknowledge the limitations of reason without at all declaring its futility. I have written this book, then, from the point of view of a Christian humanist. When I speak of religious myth, I do not mean to imply either its truth or its falsehood, for I use the term to mean the effort of the primitive, the poetic, or the religious mind to reach beyond the known and the knowable in its search for understanding. I do not think that science has disproved the Christian myth or that there is any likelihood that it will do so, nor do I agree with those who believe that recent changes in physics validate it.

Philosophically, I suppose I am nearer to being a Whiteheadian than anything else. Critically, I assume that there may be a fruitful union between philosophic and "close" criticism, that the two need not be, as they have usually been in our time, at odds. Linguistically, I assume that some such statement of the nature of language as that given in W. M. Urban's *Language and Reality* (with which, nevertheless, I do not wholly agree) is the correct one. That is to say, I shall not argue but shall simply assume the error of any behaviorist theory of language which would omit purpose, value, and mind from its description; and likewise, necessarily, I shall assume the error of any simple bifurcation of language into "emotive" and "referential" functions, for this oversimplification was a result of the behaviorist approach to the problems of language.

I assume further that poetry is not primarily a "criticism of life," and that criticism is not therefore a criticism of a criticism of life. But I also assume that poetry is not

limited to "emotive" language or to the manipulation of
"attitudes" that have no external reference. I assume that
it is an art and that its form of symbolism, closely related
to but not identical with the symbolism of ordinary discourse and also related to the symbolic languages of music
and painting, conveys something that we are justified in
calling valid knowledge. I assume that one of the chief
ways in which poetry is distinguished from logical, scientific, or utilitarian prose is by its tendency to create a
response of the complete sensibility rather than just the
reason or the practical interests or the emotions. And I use
"sensibility" to signify one's total way of responding and
ability to respond to the environment—which means that
sensibility is not just a matter of emotion, and certainly
not simply of reason, but is emotionally tinged reason and
reasonable emotion and what is called insight or intuition:
in short, awareness, the total complex awareness, physical,
psychological, and spiritual, emotional and reasonable,
with which we are able to respond to the world. (The kind
of sensibility we have determines the kind of experience
that is available to us; and experience is not all emotional.)

I assume further that facts and values, though they are
logically separate aspects of reality—so that, for instance, a
statement of what *is* is never automatically equivalent to a
statement of what *ought* to be—do not, as in the usual
modern outlook, belong to two separate and unequal
realms, the one objective and the other subjective, but
that facts become values when seen in their relation to
man and purpose and that values are always facts and are
indeed the most important kind of facts with which man
has to deal. I assume therefore, and finally, that questions
of belief are relevant in an examination of poetry and to

assert that they are not is to limit criticism in the same way and for the same reasons that Mr. Richards earlier in his career would have had us limit poetry.

This book is then an essay in philosophical criticism —*philosophical,* not *ideological,* for I do not wish to beg the question of the truth or falsity of the ideas I shall treat by using a coinage that drags along with it its whole nominalist, materialist, Marxist background. But it is not a study of the beliefs of the poets as such. I do not know of any compelling reason why we should be more interested in the beliefs of poets than we are in those of politicians and generals. Rather, I have tried always to see how belief is embodied in form and form is the substantial articulation of belief, to examine the work of certain poets against the background of modern science and philosophy on the assumption that ideally and ultimately "content" and "form" in poetry are one. The concentration of most of the new critics on rather narrowly defined questions of texture and structure, while in the past it has probably been a source of strength, permitting intensive study, may soon appear to be also a source of weakness, one of the causes of the frequent narrowness, the almost isolationist purity of the conclusions of some of the best of the critics, just as the concentration on matters of only peripheral significance of many literary scholars is a source of the frequent irrelevance of scholarship. However that may be, and even if criticism comes eventually to seem to be the chief contribution of the recent past to literature, I think we are approaching the end of a phase in criticism, as Mr. Eliot thinks we are in poetry. Just what the newer criticism should become if it is not to stagnate and so eventually be replaced by some activity quite different is anybody's guess. My own is that it should become more philosophically self-conscious, more aware of its ultimate assumptions and implications. Only thus, I think, can it find the new insights and methods necessary if it is not to become a progressively sterile application of fixed techniques of analysis to works ever more minor and unrewarding. The insights afforded by philosophical criticism and those afforded by close criticism actually can, I believe, be made to serve a common end, which is a more adequate understanding and a juster evaluation of literary works than can be attained by either alone. Whether this study demonstrates the possibility of such a blending of philosophical and close criticism is of course another matter entirely; but that such demonstrations should continually be attempted seems to me clear.

The plan of organization I have followed is first to state briefly the chief problems involved, then to examine in some detail the work of six representative modern American poets—I have taken the liberty of counting Mr. Eliot as an American poet—and finally to disengage and reconsider the themes common to the six separate studies. The method is in a sense circular: like the method of most of Emerson's essays, it would allow an indefinite expansion of content. But this is an opportunity of which I have not chosen to take advantage. For though a number of other poets invite the same sort of approach—Wallace Stevens is one of them, and W. H. Auden another—to extend the study in this way would not, I think, in the end lead to very different conclusions.

For the conclusions which I reach, although I have called this an essay in philosophical criticism, I claim no *philosophical* importance whatever. Unfortunately, I am neither a scientist nor a philosopher, and I am sure that those of my philosophic friends with whom I now disagree will continue to disagree quite as heartily if they chance to read this work. In those parts of the text where I turn from specific poems to discuss ideas in the abstract, I do so as critic and literary historian, trying simply to record and understand and clarify the ideas and to relate them to the poetry itself, not as one competent to engage in philosophic debate with professional philosophers. Rightly or wrongly, I take the ideas of the poets as seriously as their verse seems to demand. Most of my colleagues, on the other hand, particularly those in fields other than literature, seem to feel very superior indeed to Mr. Eliot in their understanding of the world, and perhaps even farther removed in wisdom from Hart Crane and E. A. Robinson, who did not have Mr. Eliot's advantage of a manner calculated to inspire awe. My colleagues tell me that the "mystical" and "absolutist" and "obscurantist" positions of the poets are not "intellectually respectable." I am not convinced that respectability is an adequate criterion of truth, but I am not prepared to argue the point seriously and formally, partly because to do so would require this whole book and more for the treatment of a matter that should be merely preliminary. I can only hope that a sufficient number of my basic assumptions are shared, or partly shared, to make a common ground of agreement from which to start the task which this study attempts: to throw some light on the nature of modern American poetry by viewing it against a backdrop of science and scientific philosophy. Those who are in total disagreement with the majority of the assumptions I have listed will probably not find the work rewarding. Such readers will probably find more profit in the scholarly, factual, and largely non-critical articles on science and the poets that I have published in the learned journals.

Acknowledgments of indebtedness I can make very briefly and yet, I believe, adequately. This is not a piece of "research" writing, but a great deal of research, as distinguished from critical analysis, has gone into it. Most of this research was done by my wife before a growing family imposed more pressing duties. I am grateful to the University of Kansas City for its system of sabbatical leaves which enabled me to write in an atmosphere where there was a minimum of distraction. Two of my undergraduate teachers at Middlebury College had more to do with the original growth of the interests and attitudes that led to this work than anyone from whom I have learned since: the late Vernon C. Harrington, a great teacher and a wise, gentle, and good man, introduced me to philosophy; and Reginald L. Cook, the most stimulating teacher of American literature I have known, showed me at a crucial moment that there was more to literature than the dreary biological and historical irrelevancies that made up the usual stock in trade of teachers of literature when I was in college. The present study is an attempt, inadequate I am sure but not misguided I hope, to blend fruitfully the philosophic and aesthetic interests stimulated more by these two than by any others.

HYATT HOWE WAGGONER

Kansas City, Missouri
  August 2, 1950

Acknowledgments

I am deeply grateful to the following publishers, who graciously granted me permission to quote certain passages from the copyrighted works of the six poets I discuss in detail:

The Macmillan Company, for E. A. Robinson's *Cavender's House* (copyright 1929 by Mr. Robinson), *King Jasper, Nicodemus* (copyright 1932 by Mr. Robinson), *The Man Against the Sky* (copyright 1916, 1944, by Mr. Robinson), and *Selected Letters;*

Henry Holt and Company, for Robert Frost's *Collected Poems,* 1949 (especially "A Winter Eden," "On a Tree Fallen Across the Road," "Sand Dune," "Riders," "West Running Brook," "Triple Bronze," "Any Size We Please," "Bursting Rapture," "The Night Light," "A Masque of Mercy," "A Leaf Treader," "A Drumlin Woodchuck," "At Woodward's Gardens");

Harcourt, Brace and Company, for T. S. Eliot's *Collected Poems—1909–1935, The Family Reunion, Four Quartets* (especially "The Dry Salvages"), and *Selected Essays;*

Random House, for Robinson Jeffers' *Dear Judas, The Women of Point Sur,* and *Selected Poems* (especially "Margrave");

Houghton Mifflin Company, for Archibald MacLeish's *Poems, 1924–1933* (especially "Seafarer," "Immortal Helix," "Verses for a Centennial," "Land's End," "Selene Afterwards," "Signature for Tempo," "The

Hamlet," "You, Andrew Marvell," "Einstein," "Epistle to Be Left in the Earth," and "Conquistador");

Liveright Publishing Corporation, for *The Collected Poems of Hart Crane* (especially "Modern Poetry," "Voyages II," and "The Bridge").

I should like also to acknowledge my indebtedness to these publishers for permission to quote from the works listed: Cambridge University Press, for Sir James Jeans, *The Mysterious Universe,* and Sir Arthur S. Eddington, *New Pathways in Science;* the University of Chicago Press, for Alfred North Whitehead, *Nature and Life;* Harcourt, Brace and Company, for John Crowe Ransom, *God Without Thunder,* and T. E. Hulme, *Speculations;* Harper and Brothers, for Lincoln Barnett, *The Universe and Dr. Einstein,* and John B. Watson, *The Ways of Behaviorism;* Harvard University Press, for Suzanne K. Langer, *Philosophy in a New Key;* Houghton Mifflin Company, for John Burroughs, *The Light of Day;* Kegan Paul, Trench, Trubner, and Company and the Orthological Institute (London), for Watson and MacDougall, *The Battle of Behaviorism,* and I. A. Richards, *Science and Poetry;* W. W. Norton and Company, for Bertrand Russell, *The Scientific Outlook* and *Mysticism and Logic;* The Macmillan Company, for Alfred North Whitehead, *Science and the Modern World,* and W. M. Urban, *Language and Reality;* Charles Scribner's Sons, for Reinhold Niebuhr, *The Nature and Destiny of Man,* and *The Collected Essays of John Peale Bishop;* and Yale University Press, for Herman Weyl, *The Open World.*

I am also grateful to the editor of *The University of Kansas City Review* for permission to reprint a portion of Chapter One.

Contents

Prefatory Note: Origins, Assumptions,
    Intentions *page* VII

Acknowledgments XVII

I. Poets, Test Tubes, and the Heel of Elohim
    1. Divergence of Ways 3
    2. Science and Value 5
    3. Poetry and Value 9
    4. The Tension and the Problem 15

II. E. A. Robinson: The Cosmic Chill
    1. The Crucial Question 18
    2. The Antagonist 24
    3. "The Man Against the Sky" 29
    4. The Effect of the Revelations 37

III. Robert Frost: The Strategic Retreat
    1. Storm Fear 41
    2. The Response 45
    3. Denials and Affirmations 50
    4. The Craft as Expression 56
    5. "The Armful" 58

IV. T. S. Eliot: At the Still Point
    1. Three Ways 61
    2. Philosophy as Preparation 63
    3. Science Condemned and Used 73
    4. A Poet in a Scientific Age 82

5. "The Dry Salvages" 90
6. Naturalism and Supernaturalism 99

V. Robinson Jeffers: Here Is Reality
   1. A Poetry Powerful and Real 105
   2. Aspects of Reality 107
   3. Form as Experience 114
   4. "Margrave" 121
   5. What Science Says 129

VI. Archibald MacLeish: The Undigested Mystery
   1. An Aspect of Eternity 133
   2. The Sense of Infinity and the
      Unanswered Question 136
   3. Were There Not Words? 140
   4. An Image of the World 151

VII. Hart Crane: Beyond All Sesames of Science
   1. My Hand in Yours 155
   2. The Logic of Ecstasy 159
   3. Lead Me Past Logic 166
   4. The Broken Parabola 171
   5. A Passage to India 190

VIII. Science and Poetry: Conclusions
   1. Language, Myth, and Metaphysic 193
   2. The Defense of Poetry 204
   3. Form and Substance 210
   4. Poetry as Document 214

Index 221

The Heel of Elohim

The habit of art is the habit of enjoying vivid values.
ALFRED NORTH WHITEHEAD

I. Poets, Test Tubes, and The Heel of Elohim

> *If a scientific civilization is to be a good civilization, it is necessary that increase in knowledge should be accompanied by increase in wisdom. I mean by wisdom a right conception of the ends of life. This is something that science in itself does not provide.*
> —BERTRAND RUSSELL *in* The Scientific Outlook

1. *Divergence of Ways*

Several years ago, early in the last war, we began to hear about the emergence of "foxhole religion," alleged by some to be a healthy sign of a much-needed religious revival, by others to be a temporary and not particularly edifying manifestation of fear psychology. Soldiers, we read, who had never been to church began to pray; aviators attributed the appearance of sea birds to Providence.

And the news, whether we read it with approval, disapproval, or mere amusement, did not come as such a surprise as it would have fifteen years earlier. For we had become accustomed through the preceding decade to books by famous scientists proving that science was not materialistic, by philosophers creating systems compatible with faith, by laymen discovering the church. A number of our young literary intellectuals had renounced the world; two at least had entered monasteries. Aldous Huxley had been assuring us for several years that time must have a stop, and Reinhold Niebuhr, arguing that the only

3

remedy for futility was Christian orthodoxy, seemed to many to be the philosopher whose influence might succeed that of the pragmatists.

The signs of this "new failure of nerve," as John Dewey has somewhat scornfully termed the increased interest in religion among the intellectuals, have been widely apparent only in the last ten years or so. But thirty years before Dr. Link announced his rediscovery of religion, thirty years before it had become a commonplace that our technical knowledge had outrun our moral wisdom, most of our best poets were viewing science and all its works with alarm. They were calling for not less knowledge of means but more knowledge of ends. They were asking ultimate questions and turning, frequently, to religion for the answers. It was indeed some forty years or more ago that Yeats and Robinson and Robert Frost, the elder masters of the poetry of our century, began rebelling against our scientific civilization; and each succeeding poetic generation has seemed equally allergic to a culture that proudly claims natural science as its base and semantics as its apex.

Yet the fundamental patterns of our society have probably been even less affected by the attitudes of the poets than the later lives of most of the soldiers have been altered by foxhole piety. Though even *Time* and *Life* have recently had a change of heart and many former Marxists have changed their creeds, the secular, scientific, and positivistic foundations of our culture remain unshaken. It is an interesting question, then, why so many of the poets have so long been concerned with religious and metaphysical questions which it has only recently become fashionable to be concerned with. Why have so many of them

4

displayed an attitude toward science compounded of fear and condescension and distaste? Why have they so consistently, and for so long, preferred "semantic blurbs" and emotive noises to the precise referential language of science and sense? When nearly every well-educated and well-adjusted man in our age is a relativist, why do most of the poets write as though they were absolutists of some sort, or aspired to be? Though the divergence of ways between the poets and their scientific society seems a little less great today than it did several decades ago, it is still great enough to give poets something of the appearance and the role of strangers in our society.

2. *Science and Value*

For ever since the Renaissance, when leeches counted the ribs of cadavers and were amazed to discover that, contrary to sound reasoning based on Biblical evidence, men have the same number of ribs on both sides (so that God must have replaced in Adam the rib which he removed and used to make Eve), Western man has been more and more concerned with the seen and the tangible and with the abstract systems which a specialized group, the scientists, have built on the evidence gathered by the senses or, in recent physics, deduced mathematically and checked experimentally. The unseen, the nonmaterial, apparently incapable of practical use and further discredited by the failure of its special champions to meet successfully the challenge of the scientists, was long ago relegated, for all practical purposes, to the limbo of the fancy, there to be dealt with by priests, professors of the humanities, and poets.

By the middle of the nineteenth century science had gone beyond its simple—and quite understandable—disinterest in the presentiments of intuition and had definitely proved, so its most enthusiastic and popular interpreters thought, that not only metaphysical and intangible notions but tangible experience as well had to be discarded as unreal or merely subjective. The story of this denial of a large part of man's experience because a smaller part seemed to demand it is long and complicated and it has been told in detail by philosophic historians of science and philosophers of history; but the essence of it, which is all I am trying to suggest, lies in the banishing of values from reality. "Finally, values took flight altogether, and the nineteenth century witnessed nihilistic doctrines which completely severed the realm of values from the realm of facts—the one unreal, the other worthless."[1] Mass and velocity, it seemed, were absolutely real, were facts which no one would dispute, but such things as the sound of a dog barking or of the Jupiter symphony, the redness of the rose and the taste of pickles, had a highly doubtful status, existing, if they could be said to exist at all, only in the mind, as a species of illusion; and holiness was, scientifically, hocus-pocus.

And science, succeeding in the realm where it sought success, was believed. Philosophies were built on its implications, systems were contrived to explain its unique access to truth, magazines and societies were formed to spread the new gospel and to belabor the unconvinced.[2]

[1] George Morgan, Jr., "Whitehead's Theory of Value," *International Journal of Ethics,* Vol. XLVII (April, 1937), 308.

[2] The fact that *scientism* was the chief popular philosophy of the educated and the half-educated in the later nineteenth century could

On positivism (which, in its classic form, declares that only scientific evidence is real evidence, that credence can be given only to the "publicly demonstrable") and on materialistic naturalism (which starts by accepting positivism and goes on to show, on undeniably adequate grounds, that science has never yet uncovered any nonmaterial cause, that everything that science has investigated through the centuries has been found to be explainable, if at all, mechanistically)—on these two philosophic twins sired by science our culture has been built.

And on these two concepts it continues to rest, somewhat uneasily these days to be sure, somewhat shaken by the explosions of a world apparently bent on blowing itself to pieces by utilizing "the miracles of science," increasingly uncertain of what the true "moral teachings of science" are, but reassured continually by those who have kept faith in the religion of science without loss of nerve. Harlow Shapley, for instance, in an article in *Harper's* reminds us that science is not simply a body of knowledge, that it is not even just a method: it is—and he tells us that we all know this—"a basic way of life, more inclusive of all the arts of living and knowing than the schoolbooks have told us." Like the famous scientists on a Sunday afternoon national radio broadcast several years ago, Mr. Shapley believes that the way to the "fuller and more fruitful life" may be discovered only by sci-

easily be documented at great length. To those acquainted with the history of thought it does not need documentation. An interesting and valuable monograph on the history of popular delusion could be written from the files of *Popular Science Monthly* in the eighteen nineties alone. No one has ever calculated the number of popular books published during the nineties with titles like *The Fairyland of Science, The Moral Teachings of Science, Miracles of Science,* and so on, but the subject is worth a long footnote in the history of ideas.

7

ence. Scientists, he said after the recent war, not states-men, should plan the peace and organize the world. And Mr. Shapley's voice as it comes in over the radio is calm and assured; there is no urgency in it, for he knows that most of us either already agree or can easily be convinced. Nineteenth-century scientism is far from dead, despite the trend of our younger intellectuals.

Now recent philosophic interpretations of science, and particularly of the new physics, have, to be sure, made nineteenth-century scientific materialism seem as out of date as a haircloth sofa, at least among the major scientists, who write the books we laymen read. (One suspects that most high-school and many college teachers of science still have more in common with Tyndall—who said he could understand nothing in science of which he could not construct a mechanical model—than they have with Heisenberg and Weyl and Planck and Whitehead.) The scientists have at last, we are relieved to read, found a place for man in the world. We may at least tentatively, if we wish, cease worrying about being in an "alien uni-verse." Some famous scientists have even come to agree with their semiscientific cousins, the sociologists, that val-ues, those elusive intangibles we live by, are not unreal at all but should immediately become the subject of sci-entific study. Eagerly we await the day when Dr. X, psy-chologist, will submit incontrovertible proof that Mo-zart's music is more beautiful than Beethoven's and *ought* to be preferred to the deaf master's. More eagerly still, though perhaps a little uneasily, we anticipate the public demonstration by Dr. Y, political scientist, that we *ought* to vote the Democratic—or could it be the Republican?—ticket. Still more gratifying will be the publication of decisive proof, no doubt by a sociologist, that hedonism is a better way of life than asceticism.

Some of the newer interpretations of science, then, tend to agree that values are real, important, and purely relative; they disagree on whether or not science can become an arbiter of values. But whichever is the case, science and reliable knowledge, we are assured, are synonymous. Only the scientist, then, has knowledge that can be depended upon to help us. And what the scientist knows has thus far in the world's history always been concerned with matters of fact, not with matters of value. (To deny that there is any difference at all between the two—any difference for instance between the subject and the concern of physics and the subject and the concern of poetry or painting or religion or morality—is to descend to irrationality in an effort to defend the prestige of science.) Even now that "matter" has evaporated into "energy patterns," physicists must cease being physicists and become amateur theologians or philosophers if they wish to write about the status of man's values in the "mysterious universe." Or again, even if we should persuade ourselves that the famous principle of indeterminacy proves—by some wild *non sequitur*—the freedom of the will, the question would still remain, at least until the scientists settle it, if they can do so before an atomic total war makes it unnecessary, what shall we *will?*

3. *Poetry and Value*

Now the poets have been concerned with this problem— the place of value in a world of fact—all through the last fifty years while scientism has been riding the wave. They

9

were concerned with it long before it became the fashion for literary intellectuals to be concerned with it. They were concerned with it before, and they have been no less concerned with it after, the development of quantum physics. While the positivistic and naturalistic spirit has been penetrating ever deeper and deeper into all the literate strata of our population, the poets have never ceased to address themselves to problems wholly outside the province and traditionally inconsistent with the outlook of natural science. Indeed, the poets seem often to imply that the statement of the fact-value problem should be reversed to read: the place of fact in a world of value. Perhaps one of the reasons why the writing of poetry is one of the least profitable of all the seldom-profitable learned occupations these days is that so many of the poets are concerned with matters that almost every sound, well-educated, and well-adjusted citizen knows are either unreal, or unimportant—or just about to be dealt with and disposed of in the laboratory or the sociologist's questionnaire.

For no age, not even the middle of the seventeenth century, has produced poetry more preoccupied with religious and metaphysical issues. The poetic sensibility of our age could almost be said to be a religious sensibility. Yeats escaped from meaninglessness into occultism. Robinson searched for the Light and tried to adapt to an age of positivistic naturalism the "far-sent Message of the years." Eliot long ago took the bishops convened at Lambeth to task for their willingness to compromise with the scientific spirit of the age. Hart Crane, terribly disturbed by the implications emanating from the laboratory, listened in mystic abandon to the "sounding heel" of Elohim.

Auden has gone along with Aldous Huxley and Gerald Heard in search of faith, and the work of Day Lewis and Stephen Spender exhibits an increasingly religious sensibility. Jeffers, after his show of strictly scientific materialism, seems to have found an alien God that shows Itself in the beauty of hawks and stars. Even common-sense Mr. Frost, avowedly unconcerned with things transcendental, of late years has worried the problem of Providence from almost all possible points of view, most recently from that of Job and his wife and a modern Jonah. All of which brings us back to where we started: the poets are and have been for a long time far more concerned with religious and metaphysical issues than the society in which they live and for which they write. Why?

Perhaps because poets as a group are, though some psychologists describe them as maladjusted and define art as the product of neurosis, actually better integrated than the rest of us. Ever since the ability to compose verses ceased to be a social accomplishment expected of all polished gentlemen, the craft of poetry has demanded a good deal more than technical dexterity: it has demanded "wit," or a "sense of something far more deeply interfused," or personal emotion, or prophecy, or social criticism, or an ability to tap the unconscious and reveal its secrets. It has demanded, in other words, that the poet employ all his powers, not merely his metrical skill, in his work.

Thus it may be that while the rest of us have gone on living more and more schizoid lives, the poet has been forced by public expectation and the nature of his occupation to continue being a whole man. Mr. Eliot may be right that personal emotion is undesirable in poetry, but

11

still one could make a good case, I think, for the argument that poets, Mr. Eliot himself included, have generally been more directly responsive in their work to their feelings, their intuitions, the subtle influences of the lymphatic currents, than bankers, engineers, real-estate salesmen, or machinists are in their work. They have actually concerned themselves very largely, that is—whether they should have done so or not—with those very promptings and secret undebatable sentiments which science and semantics define as meaningless.

And since all men in full possession of their natural human powers, including behavioristic semanticists, hunger for meaning, for the very kind of meaning that cannot, in scientific terms, exist, the poets, attending to those intuitions and emotional convictions which, when interpreted in myth or metaphysics or theology, alone seem to them capable of supplying general meaning, have allowed an aspect of their consciousness which other men today suppress to mold their work. They have written so much religious and metaphysical poetry because they have tended to remain whole men, working not with just a part of themselves, as the assembly-line worker uses chiefly his hands and a banker chiefly his conscious reason and the promptings of the profit motive, but with all they are and know.

Or again—that "why?" prompts many conjectures— the modern poetry-reading public expects the poet to deal with sensate experience, with sight and sound, smell and taste, the immediate *feel* of things. It expects that abstractions will be expressed concretely, particularized, that even in didactic poetry the reasoning will be structurally dependent on evoked concrete experience. Mr.

Eliot formulated the law of the "objective correlative" and substantially altered modern poetry and criticism by doing so, but many of those unacquainted with *The Sacred Wood* have made essentially the same demand. The poet today then, even more than in some periods in the past, must constantly concern himself with the immediately presented data of experience, not with ramifying abstractions and systems of logic or of utility, not with formulae for computing stress, not with interest-rate tables. He must concern himself with Prufrock's feeling of indecision and the look of his thinning hair, with the glossy smoothness of the apple's skin, with the cry of the children in the ruins.

But concrete experience has meaning—indeed, it has form, has existence—only in terms of values. And valuing one thing more means valuing another less. Even on the rudimentary level this is so: the phenomenon of attention, without which experience could not be said to exist because it would be, if anything, an indescribable blur, means exclusion as much as it means concentration. We respond to meaningful patterns, and we contribute a part of the meaning. We interpret even as we see, not simply after we have seen. Awareness is a dynamic and purposeful activity, not, as the behaviorists would have it, a mechanistic responsiveness to atomistic stimuli. But to what sound do we listen, of what sight are we aware? To exclude and to admit—unconsciously for the most part, of course—is to place values on things, or better, to see values in things. But discrete values always imply a unifying value, lesser values a greater value, for value-objects compete for our attention, conflict, and exclude each other. Which shall we prefer? So poets listen for the

13

sounding heel of Elohim, hoping that it will tell them which are the good, the right, the preferable value-objects, hoping that if they hear it aright it will give direction and final meaning to experience. Having found that science does not in fact, despite the pretensions of the sociologists and the hopes of the instrumentalists, solve value problems, and having found that experience is instinct with value, the poets begin to talk in semantic blurbs, begin to search for a supreme and unifying set of values in metaphysics or theology.

Finally, some men appear to have direct experiences of a special sort which seem to them to have religious significance. They feel the presence of unseen powers, they sense, with Wordsworth, a transcendent unity behind the welter of things, or they see, like Blake, an angel in the branches of a tree. Most men appear not to have these disturbing, comforting, or just puzzling experiences; but some men do, and in our day, instead of going into the church, they often become poets. If they are the sort of people for whom such experiences are frequent—and if frequent they can hardly be other than important—they are unlikely, for obvious reasons, to go into one of the better-adjusted, more typical, and better-paid occupations. They may become academic philosophers or professors of English, novelists, ministers or priests—or poets. So poetry, which in our day attracts such people (the mechanisms of escape and regression, we hear the psychologist murmur), is religious and metaphysical in a culture in which, for the dominant minority, religion and metaphysics are matters of indifference.

4. *The Tension and the Problem*

"Art," writes W. M. Urban, "is a special revelation of reality whose nature and structure are determined by the principle of value appreciation." And poetry, he continues, "always speaks of 'souls,' even when paradoxically, as in naturalistic poetry, it denies their existence." The language of poetry says many things implicitly, "but one thing it always says, namely, that human life and man are unique, free, and self-determining parts of nature."[3]

Now it is the conviction of the dominant minority today that values are merely individual preferences, that, superficially considered, they are matters of taste, more profoundly analyzed, matters of accident or necessity, whichever we choose to name it, originating in chains of determinism converging on the present time and place from past times and places through the realms of nature that we roughly distinguish as heredity and environment. A relativist, the modern man knows that values are relative to time and place and the state of one's digestion; as a relativist he realizes that if the phrase "a special revelation of reality" is applied to poetry, it can only mean that poetry, by revealing the mores and individual preferences of men, supplies data for anthropology. (Then, of course, it is not a "special" revelation, only another revelation, like newspaper stories and radio programs and prehistoric cooking utensils.) But this is not what the major poets of past or present have thought they were revealing.

Again, the enlightened modern man knows that "souls" do not exist. Antique ages were concerned with the cure of souls; we have learned to redirect the fixations

[3] *Language and Reality* (London, 1939), 489, 494, 495.

15

and condition the reflexes. No well-educated person out-side the ministry can speak or write today of the soul without embarrassment or defiance or humor. Even Mr. Urban, concerned to combat positivist and behaviorist theories of language, must enclose the word in quotation marks so that he may not be thought naïve. But he is quite right in saying that poetry treats souls even when its prose content denies them. And he might have added, had his primary interest been poetry rather than the philosophy of language, that an examination of poetry shows that to the extent that it does not do so, it fails as poetry. (The same statement might be made about the novel. If Zola had been consistently able to achieve his expressed aim of treating people as *things,* his novels would be merely curious expressions of a false philosophy.)

The concept of a *soul* shares with that of a *person* the idea of freedom, of self-direction, and so of responsibility. (Not of course absolute freedom, just enough to make room for the concept of responsibility.) We do not hold lunatics and infants responsible for their actions. Yet we think we know, as moderns, that man is not free, that he is the product of his genes and his conditioning and the vagaries of his id. We are then as a society in the untenable position of denying freedom, yet treating man in our courts and in our ordinary daily actions as though he were free. The poets have generally not been so inconsistent. They have sought for myths which would square with the implicit declarations of their procedures as poets; they have recognized the discrepancy between their art and the outlook of their time; if, like Mr. Jeffers, they have chosen during the recent past to be contemporary in their belief at all costs, they have declared the futility

16

or the absurdity of poetry. Although the language of poetry may not be essentially and always, as Mr. Cleanth Brooks insists, the language of paradox, the poets seem to be far quicker than the society of which they are a part to recognize a paradox when one appears.

If this tension between the facts of science and the facts of poetry has actually existed in our time, as I believe I can show, then it must profoundly have affected modern poetry. All the definitions of poetry that I have ever seen have been inadequate in some respect, so I shall not attempt another; but certainly, among other things, poetry is a formal aesthetic articulation in words of the sensibility of the poet. And sensibility is partly the product of the historical environment. Modern poetry, then, must reflect, in its very nature as poetry, in its "forms" as well as in its "ideas," the tension between fact and value, science and poetry, that I have been trying sketchily to suggest. How has it been so affected, to what extent and in what ways? What have been the attitudes of the poets toward science? How have they treated the values revealed to them or apparently revealed—by their craft? To what extent are individual poems and the bodies of poetry of individual poets illuminated by being placed against a background of science and scientific philosophy? To what extent does the special modern quality of modern verse derive from the tension between fact and value that I have outlined? What does modern poetry say, implicitly and explicitly, about the nature of reality? These are some of the questions with which we shall be concerned in the chapters that follow.

II. E. A. Robinson:
The Cosmic Chill

*As the physical world-picture grew and tech-
nology advanced, those disciplines which rested
squarely on "rational" instead of "empirical" prin
ciples were threatened with complete extinction.
. . . The truth is that science has not fructified and
activated all human thought.*
—SUZANNE K. LANGER *in* Philosophy in a New Key

1. *The Crucial Question*

When Hawthorne in "Alice Doane's Appeal" described Salem during an ice storm and suggested
that the ice was not limited to the trees and streets in the
frozen village, he had found a symbol more perfectly
suited to his purposes than the black veil, the birthmark,
or the wedding knell. But he never used it again, preferring instead usually the laboriously conceived products of an active fancy and seldom achieving complete
and perfect expression of his sensibility.

So, too, E. A. Robinson—who felt the chill of a frozen
world as deep in the marrow as ever Hawthorne did—
was, toward the end of his life, ordinarily unable to find
the symbols he needed. His poetry gives evidence of the
paralysis of the will that affected Wakefield, though few
of his poems express it. The result is, of course, an im-
poverishment of his work which, were it not for a relatively few poems, would make it impossible to consider
him a major poet. The common, the almost unanimous

opinion that Robinson's best work was done in the short poems, and especially in the poems of the early and middle periods, seems to me justified; but no good reason for this has ever been suggested. There must have been a number of reasons why the poems to which Robinson devoted the major portion of his poetic energy during the last twenty years or so of his life are generally less satisfactory than his early and his casual poems, but one of the reasons and not the least significant will be found, I think, to be similar to that which prevented Hawthorne from completing, indeed even from satisfactorily starting, his late romances. Robinson's sympathy for Hawthorne was deep, and the parallel between them striking. The thought of each led to an impasse which paralyzed the sensibilities.

The framework of Robinson's thought was put together in the late nineteenth century, and not chiefly by the major thinkers of the age. The poet's contact with logic and philosophy in college produced a distaste for both. At the end of the century he was defending Herbert Spencer as *the* philosopher; he read William James with great distaste, felt that Santayana was bloodless, found something to admire in Schopenhauer and Nietzsche, and was impressed by Mary Baker Eddy's *Science and Health,* which seemed to him a remarkable book though he could not accept it "in detail." Notable here are both the emphases (Spencer, Schopenhauer, Nietzsche, and Mary Baker Eddy!) and the omissions or negative reactions (Bradley, Royce, Santayana, James—very nearly a list of the best philosophic minds of the day).

Unquestioning obeisance to science Robinson absorbed not only from Spencer but from the spirit of the

THE HEEL OF ELOHIM

times, whether or not he read *Popular Science Monthly,* which devoted itself to spreading Spencer's gospel. Yet at the same time he also absorbed a corrupted Emersonianism, which had become in his time and place like "common sense," an unexamined part of the furniture of the mind. So that, despite his reading of Nietzsche and Schopenhauer, his ideas have less in common with those of the major philosophers than they have with those of John Burroughs, who combined Emerson, Whitman, and Herbert Spencer in an optimistic synthesis, or John Fiske, who aspired by a positivistic method applied with a certain vagueness through nature to God. Despite his acquaintance with the work of Santayana, his early thoughts on religion reflect the popular solution of the time in Protestant America: drop theology with positive benefit to religion, a solution he might have found learnedly put forth in the nineties by Andrew Dickson White's massive *History of the Warfare of Science with Theology in Christendom.* His early poems express contemporary popular "advanced" thought, without the customary enthusiasm for the conclusions of the thought.[1]

---

[1] This seems to me to be the only conclusion one can reach despite Miss Estelle Kaplan's attempt to trace the influence of several major philosophers in Robinson's work (*Philosophy in the Poetry of Edwin Arlington Robinson* [New York, 1940]). Evidence of the nature and extent of Robinson's reading may be found in Hermann Hagedorn, *Edwin Arlington Robinson* (New York, 1938), *Selected Letters of Edwin Arlington Robinson* (New York, 1940), and Denham Sutcliffe (ed.), *Untriangulated Stars* (Cambridge, Mass., 1947), which are the chief sources of the facts I have just summarized. There seems to be a tendency for studies of Robinson's thought either to demonstrate the obvious or to end in silliness, with an inverse proportion between the elaborateness of the study and the value of its conclusions. One of the most sensible of such studies is also one of the earliest and briefest: Chapter 5 of Lloyd Morris's *The Poetry of Edwin Arlington Robinson* (New York, 1923). Of con-

E. A. Robinson

It is more enlightening, then, to compare his early thinking with that of the popular philosophers and minor spokesmen of the age than with that of the best minds. True, he knew James's "will to believe," was fully aware of the neutral world described by science which formed one strand of Santayana's thought, and was an idealist by inclination as was Royce; but much more evident in his poetry is that state of mind described by John Burroughs at the end of the century in *The Light of Day*. "Feeling, emotion," wrote Burroughs, "falls helpless before the revelations of science. The universe is going its own way with no thought of us. . . . This discovery sends the cosmic chill, with which so many of us are familiar in these days."

Burroughs might have been writing of the effect of scientific doctrines on any of a great number of literary people before or after Robinson's time, on Tennyson or Arnold, on MacLeish or Aldous Huxley; again, the passage might be from Krutch's *The Modern Temper* (1929) instead of from *The Light of Day* (1900), so generally true is it. But there are several reasons why it makes a particularly good starting point for a discussion of Robinson. First, the "revelations of science" lead Burroughs to a conception of an alien universe, not to a new conception of man. Purpose and meaning are gone *from the world;* the universe is fully revealed by physics and chemistry. So in Robinson's poetry the effect of science is chiefly what we should expect it to be in a poet reared in the century dominated by advances in biology and physics. It

siderable value are F. I. Carpenter's "Tristam the Transcendent," *New England Quarterly,* Vol. XI, No. 3 (September, 1938), 501–23, and Floyd Stovall's "The Optimism Behind Robinson's Tragedies," *American Literature,* Vol. X, No. 1 (March, 1938), 1–23.

remained for the younger poets to be affected by the sciences developed in our century, especially psychology and sociology, and to impale themselves upon the other horn of the naturalistic dilemma, the dehumanization of man.

Second, the revelations of science, Burroughs says, paralyze feeling and chill the mind. Burroughs's language here is apt, though perhaps somewhat too rhetorical. T. S. Eliot and others who have deplored the "dissociation of sensibility" of the nineteenth century have not always set the fact in its historic context. When one is faced with a totally hopeless situation, one may continue to think, but the thinking will be without purpose so far as the situation is concerned; if the situation is all-inclusive, one's thought will take on the character of day-dreaming. One may also continue to feel, but the emotion will not issue in action nor will it activate thought. The road from thought to action leads through emotion, and from emotion to sane action through thought; and either course requires a sense of purpose if the transit is to be completed. To the extent that an age thinks it has discovered ultimate meaninglessness, to the extent that it has lost a sense of security, it will be characterized by dissociation of sensibility. Neurosis is an individual matter, no doubt, but ages and peoples may exhibit neurotic symptoms.[2]

Robinson's poetry is that of a man whose mind and heart are at odds. His didactic poems are ordinarily his poorest work, and the more ambitious his effort in this direction the weaker the result. When "The Man Against the Sky" again and again breaks down into rhymed prose,

[2] Erich Fromm, *Escape from Freedom* (New York, 1941).

the failure is not a "technical" one but the result of a
breakdown of thought and feeling, an impasse of the soul.
If the philosophic passages in his long narrative poems
are frequently thin and verbose, unconvincing and even
tedious, it is because they are most often on the theme
of ultimate meaning and on this theme Robinson could
only think and feel by turns.

Yet he worried the theme throughout his whole poetic
career. His best poems—"Hillcrest," "Eros Turannos,"
"Isaac and Archibald," "Dark Hills," "New England,"
"Miniver Cheevy," and many others—concern it only indirectly or not at all. But from *The Children of the Night*
to *King Jasper* much of his best effort was devoted to this
theme which he was least able to handle. Further to define the theme and the feeling with which for Robinson
it was surrounded, I shall again avail myself of quotation.
Lord Russell's essay "A Free Man's Worship" has been
called by Mr. Eliot a piece of sentimental rhetoric, and
from any point of view resembling Mr. Eliot's it no doubt
deserves the description; but it expresses precisely, yet in
terms general enough to fit both the early and late poems,
the course of thought and the state of feeling which dominated Robinson's poetry from beginning to end. The
question with which the passage ends is the question
which Robinson devoted himself to attempting to answer
in all of his philosophic poems:

That man is the product of causes that had no prevision
of the end they were achieving; that his origin, his growth, his
hopes and fears, his loves and beliefs are but the outcome of
accidental collocations of atoms; that no fire, no heroism, no
intensity of thought and feeling, can preserve an individual
life beyond the grave; that all the labors of the ages, all the

devotion, all the inspiration, all the noonday brightness of human genius, are destined to extinction in the vast death of the solar system, and that the whole temple of man's achievement must inevitably be buried beneath the debris of a universe in ruins—all these things, if not quite beyond dispute, are yet so nearly certain, that no philosophy which rejects them can hope to stand. Only within the scaffolding of these truths, only on the firm foundation of unyielding despair, can the soul's habitation henceforth be safely built.

How, in such an alien and inhuman world, can so powerless a creature as Man preserve his aspirations untarnished?[3]

2. *The Antagonist*

That the unhappy revelations of science did indeed provide Robinson with the chief stimulus to his thinking and determine the main course of his philosophic poems need not be demonstrated to anyone thoroughly acquainted with the whole body of Robinson's work, though it may not be apparent from a reading of the usual anthology pieces. Again, though an adequate biography of the poet remains to be written and not all of his letters have been published, there is sufficient external evidence to show that Robinson read the usual books on science and scientific philosophy and discussed the subject frequently with his friends. What is more to the point is the frequency and nature of his allusions to science in his poems.

It is clear upon even casual inspection that the significance of science for Robinson in the nineties and the earliest years of this century lay in the fact that it was in

[3] The essay, first published in 1903, may be found in Russell's *Mysticism and Logic* (London, 1923).

conflict with "the creeds." Just which religious doctrines
were disproved by science, Robinson never made clear in
his poetry, nor is it likely that he thought much about it.
It simply seemed to him as to others that science had cut
the ground out from under any supernaturalist interpretation of life and the world. So the "obsolescent creeds"
must go; only the "common creed of common sense," the
doing of "his will," could stand in the face of the new
knowledge. Yet there must, he thought, be immortality;
if there were not another chance, it would be better if
we had never been born. One must somehow maintain
confidence in "Life's purposeful and all-triumphant sail-
ing." There must be a God, and He must be Love, and
just. "It is the faith within the fear That holds us to the
life we curse." The chief impression one gets from Robinson's earliest work is that he is whistling in what he
customarily wrote as "the Dark."

The faith he longed for and at times thought he had
was a sort of Emersonian romantic naturalism. "So let us
in ourselves revere The Self which is the universe." God
thrilled the first atom with a mystic touch. Evolution
could—must—be interpreted idealistically and man
would move forward into the light as he put off old superstitions. F. I. Carpenter has shown us the transcendental
elements in Robinson's work, and we are grateful for the
demonstration; but it seems to me that we should expect
Robinson to adopt the Emersonian line and should be
surprised only if we were to discover that he did not, the
state of liberal opinion in late nineteenth-century New
England being what it was. It would be quite possible,
though I think not entirely worth while, to trace the correspondences between Robinson's early poetry and the

sort of thought that Emerson's influence had contributed to so strongly, the "religion of humanity" of Robert Ingersoll, for instance, the idealism of John Fiske, and the published sermons of countless liberal Protestant preachers of the day. The point is that Robinson's thinking on the subject in his early years is indistinguishable from popular "advanced" thinking of the time.

But Emerson's solution of saving God by identifying Him with the whole course and nature of things seemed less and less like a solution to Robinson, as to the literate public generally, as the years went by.[4] Open skepticism became more prominent in the poems than the desperate hope, which became steadily more desperate and more attentuated. Like Cavender, Robinson knew a need to believe rather than a belief:

> *And so there must be God; or if not God,*
> *A purpose or a law. Or was the world,*
> *And the strange parasites infesting it,*
> *Serpent or man or limpet, or what not,*
> *Merely a seeming-endless incident*
> *Of doom?*

More and more frequently Robinson made the characters in his long narrative poems share Cavender's sensation that he could "feel atoms moving and conspiring Against him, and death rustling in the shadows." References to the creeds diminished and the problem came to be phrased in philosophic terms. The question was now sim-

---

4 Robinson's omission of "The Children of the Night" from all editions of his *Collected Poems* is symptomatic of this shift in his opinions, as it is also of a change in his standards of taste. "The Children of the Night" is not only very weak poetry; it is also more forthright in its expression of faith than Robinson later felt able to be.

ply whether the universe was purposeful or not, whether science told all. What had once seemed like the answer, dropping theology and keeping religion, was now seen to be merely a verbal solution. What was at stake was the status of value in a world in which the "chemistry of fate" seemed quite adequate to account for everything. In the years just before World War I Robinson faced the issue fully; from then on to the end of his life he pondered the scientific "news of an ingenious mechanism" and concluded that there was no way of countering the dismaying news by argument, that there was only, as he said in *King Jasper,* the final conviction that

> *...No God*
> *No law, no purpose, could have hatched for sport*
> *Out of warm water and slime, a war for life*
> *That was unnecessary, and far better*
> *Never had been—if man, as we behold him,*
> *Is all it means.*

I shall comment shortly on the quality of the poetry in which Robinson's convictions are expressed, but what concerns us at present is the convictions themselves, insofar as it is possible to separate matter from manner—and in this kind of poetry it is possible, up to a point. The convictions can be summarized quite simply, for the ideas involved are neither complex nor profound. We must recapture the atmosphere of the mechanist-vitalist controversy to set the terms in their proper context, and that is all. Robinson is concerned with the devastating implications of materialistic naturalism, which finds purpose, value, even quality as distinguished from measureable quantity, subjective or unreal. In an era when John B.

Watson, then thought to be the leading American psychologist, was proclaiming that psychologists must start their work by ruling out the possibility of there being any soul, mind, will, purpose, or memory, Robinson was concerned to keep these entities. Humanistic knowledge must be of some real significance, but it could not be if life were "really" only "a riot of cells and chemistry," an "accident of nameless energies."

> *. . . There is more of me*
> *I hope, than a pathetic mechanism*
> *Grinding itself to nothing. Possibly not,*
> *But let me say there is.*

In an era when the universe was thought to have been revealed as a vast machine in which matter and motion were the only realities, Robinson found "a free man's worship" not enough. For him, as for so many others, knowledge was "cruel" and the need for faith great; but the "unanswered questions" remained and Robinson's faith continued to be like that of most men he knew, "whose faith, when they are driven to think of it, is mostly doubts and fears." To deny the total validity of what seemed to him the unarguable "facts" of science, he had to deny positivism. There are, he felt, areas of reality with which "myopic science" with its "inch-ruling of the infinite" cannot deal. The conviction toward which he was moving suggests Whitehead's position on the nature and results of abstraction in science, though I know of no evidence that Robinson was familiar at first hand with Whitehead's work. But his inability to formulate any clear statements about these areas left over after science has finished its work would seem to confirm not his convictions but those of the logical positivists.

I have said that the ideas in Robinson's poetry are neither complex nor profound. I should add that Robinson himself was the first to insist that they were not. In view of all the studies of his philosophy, it is interesting to note what he said in a letter written in 1930: "There is no 'philosophy' in my poetry beyond an implication of an ordered universe and a sort of deterministic negation of the general futility that appears to be the basis of rational thought." And there is a touch of pathos in his remark in a letter to a candidate for an advanced degree:

I am naturally gratified to learn that you are writing a thesis on my poetry, but I am rather sorry to learn that you are writing about my "philosophy"—which is mostly a statement of my inability to accept a mechanistic interpretation of the universe and of life. . . . I still wish that you were writing about my poetry—of which my so-called philosophy is only a small part, and probably the least important.

3. *"The Man Against the Sky"*

"The Man Against the Sky" is Robinson's most ambitious attempt to set forth his thought on ultimate problems. Although modesty and insight made him declare that his ideas were probably the least important part of his poetry, this poem, on which as much as on any other his reputation was founded, is solely concerned with ideas. In it man's destiny is examined in the light of several current outlooks; various popular philosophies and attitudes toward life are discussed and rejected. And since the spur to thought here, as elsewhere in Robinson's poetry, is the question Lord Russell asked, I shall examine the poem in some detail.

The form is very loose. Irregularly rhymed and with lines of varying length, it seems to fall logically into three main parts, but there is no formal relation between its ten verse paragraphs and the logic of its structure. The language is very general, with the abstract diction, suggestive of philosophic or polemic prose, varied here and there by generalized and frequently traditional figures. Thus the commonly accepted goals, "a kingdom and a power and a Race," are said to end in "ashes and eternal night"; *eternity, death, faith, ambition, light,* and *dark* and their modifiers make up the core of the poem. The texture is thin, the method discursive.[5] It seems to me that only Robinson's honesty and thoughtfulness save the poem from being completely uninteresting, and even

---

[5] If it were a part of my purpose here to attempt a complete evaluation of Robinson's language, I should try to show that his turn from the conventional poetic language of the late nineteenth century to a more natural language having recognizable connections with his own spoken idiom is an important part of his achievement as a poet, whereas his tendency toward the abstract discursive language of prose is often a weakness in his work. But to discuss this question would take me beyond the limits set by the purpose of this book. The question is a very difficult one, involving such problems, central in contemporary criticism, as the nature and value of didactic poetry, a problem on which Mr. Yvor Winters gives one answer while most of the other new critics give a radically different one. All that I should insist on is that Robinson's tendency to make his longer poems all argument and speculation is a very different thing from his "plain," "dry," "factual" language. That poetry is at its best when it is symbolic in its own way (not necessarily when it is "pure" or incapable of being paraphrased) has been argued not only by the new critics but by two philosophers, Susanne K. Langer and W. M. Urban. As Mr. Urban puts it in *Language and Reality* (London, 1939, p. 500), "The poet . . . does well . . . to keep to his own symbolic form. For precisely in that symbolic form an aspect of reality is given which cannot be adequately expressed otherwise. It is not true that whatever can be

these are not sufficient to make it a really distinguished poem, partly for the obvious reason that distinguished poems are not made by honesty and thoughtfulness and partly because even considered as a prose statement the poem is finally unsuccessful. But because its failure is so fully illustrative of Robinson's typical weaknesses, and because those weaknesses are closely connected with the aspects of his thought and sensibility which are my subject, I want to summarize what the poem says.

The man outlined against the sunset as he walks over the hill toward the west is any man—mankind—seen in the ultimate perspective of death. The "world on fire" against which he is outlined is at once the sunset, the conflagration of the World War I, and the universe described by science, with its live stars and dead stars, the electrical nature of matter, and so on. (And this, incidentally, is one of the few figures in the poem that have several levels of meaning.) Robinson wonders how the man approaches death. The introduction of the poem ends with the second verse paragraph.

The second part of the poem, logically divided, sets forth various attitudes toward life and death. This section keeps to the original figure of the man against the sky and relates the outlooks discussed to appropriate character types. Thus, first, the figure may be a man of unshaken faith, an anachronism in an age of doubt; or, second, a practical, unthoughtful man who has been so fortunate

---

expressed symbolically can be better expressed literally. For there *is* no literal expression, but only another kind of symbol." It seems to me that the weaknesses—though not all of the strength—in Robinson's poetry could be revealed by an analysis in terms of Mr. Allen Tate's principle of *tension* in poetry.

as never to have known the trials that would shake an instinctive faith, a natural materialist; or, third, a cynical pessimist getting a kind of pleasure out of denial of meaning, a philosophic materialist; or, fourth, a man with religious instincts who has lost his faith and is now moved to terror and despair by his vision of "the living death Assigned alike by chance To brutes and hierophants," a "world without meaning" in which "molecules" are the ultimate realities; or, last, an ambitious and worldly man who, absorbed in his pride and search for power, finds no reason to question his importance in the scheme of things and takes pride in "being what he must have been by laws Infrangible and for no kind of cause," a man who looks with his "mechanic eyes" at an "accidental universe" but is not disturbed because he cannot conceive of the world without him.

In the eighth verse paragraph, beginning "Whatever the dark road he may have taken," Robinson sums up the several types he has presented and comments on them and on life in general: "His way was even as ours." Now the center of his interest is revealed: not the types dramatically conceived but the ideas he has assigned to them. From this point on in the poem, the opening figure of the man against the sky is lost from sight; he has served his purpose as a starting point for philosophic speculation and he never reappears.

This third and purely abstract part of the poem presents Robinson's conclusions. That it does so with neither poetic richness nor prose clarity or emphasis is hardly surprising in view of the structure of the poem as I have noted it so far. First the poet mentions and rejects various current justifications of life—the capitalist and commu-

nist variants of the notion of progress, scientific humanism, evolution. Then he asks if we shall no more hear the
Word. One cannot be sure from the poem which variety
of religious enlightenment the Word represents, nor does
external evidence help very much to clarify this rather
literal but at the same time vague symbol. One thinks, of
course, of Christ as the Word, but one of Robinson's clear-
est prose statements on Christianity was made in 1896
when he wrote to his friend Arthur Gledhill, "I have
been slowly getting rid of materialism for the past year
or two, but I fear I haven't the stamina to be a Christian,
accepting Christ as either human or divine"; with which
we may compare his statement in a letter to Laura Richards written a year before his death: "Christian theology
has so thoroughly crumbled that I do not think of any
non-Roman acquaintance to whom it means anything—
and I doubt if you do." If Christianity then is out, could
the Word be just any comforting faith, any "religion"
which would supply the missing sense of purpose? Presumably so; yet it is clear that some of the faiths which
the poem has already rejected, notably communism, serve
their followers in much the same way that Christianity
serves Christians, supplying an orientation and a sense of
purpose. It is significant of the confusion in the poem that
it rejects various religions on grounds which it does not
specify and then calls for a new religion of unspecified
nature. What Robinson probably had in mind in writing
of the Word which we might or might not hear again is
somewhat more clearly indicated by another of his statements in his late letter to Mrs. Richards: "There's a non-
theological religion on the way, probably to be revealed
by science when science comes definitely to the jumping-

off place." How such a "non-theological" religion—which is to say nonrational, uninterpreted, unphilosophical, and in the last analysis undefinable—would differ from Robinson's own religious sentiment, which he found so inadequate to his needs, is not clear.[6]

The poem ends with a passage which is clearer prose than most of the earlier portions, though it is probably weaker poetry. It might perhaps be called a negative affirmation: since none of the five attitudes reviewed in the second part of the poem, nor any of the several "faiths"

[6] With this statement of Robinson's it is interesting to compare one made by Thomas Mann in 1941: "Unmistakably the spirit is today in readiness to enter upon a moral epoch, an epoch of new religious and moral knowledge and distinction of good and evil." ("Thought and Life," *The American Scholar*, Vol. X, No. 4 [Autumn, 1941], 414). The insight common to the two statements seems to me in process of being justified, but it is notable that whereas Mann predicts a genuine religious revival, with articulated "knowledge" at its core, Robinson sees the possibility only of a revival of religious emotion.

Robinson read many of the works of the philosophical scientists in his last years, and what he probably had in mind when he hoped that science would come to the rescue of intuitions no longer adequately supported by religion was something similar to the idea expressed by the famous scientist Herman Weyl several years after Robinson's death, an idea wholly typical of the newer interpretations of science at that time: "The connections between that abstract world beyond ⌈the world studied by physics⌉ and the one which I perceive is necessarily of a statistical nature. This fact, together with the new insight which modern physics affords us into the relation between subject and object, opens several ways of reconciling personal freedom with natural law. . . . We must await the further developments of science . . . before we can design a true and detailed picture of the interwoven texture of Matter, Life, and Soul. But the old classical determinism of Hobbes need not oppress us any longer." (*The Open World* [New Haven, Conn., 1932], 55.) More recently Lecomte du Nouy in his *Human Destiny* (New York, 1947) has continued a tradition now at least twenty years old by arguing from the evidence of the new physics and from the statistical nature of scientific law that a true understanding of science leads to an outlook which he calls *telefinalism*, which in turn is found to be consistent with the religious doctrines of the existence of God, of free will, of original sin, and so on.

presented in the third part, can be accepted, and since no
one today has "ever heard or ever spelt" the Word without experiencing the "fears and old surrenderings and
terrors" that beset us, the conclusion can only be considered negative in fact, despite its apparent intention of
affirming some kind of faith:

> *If after all that we have lived and thought*
> *All comes to Nought, —*
> *If there be nothing after Now,*
> *And we be nothing anyhow,*
> *And we know that, — why live?*
> *'Twere sure but weaklings' vain distress*
> *To suffer dungeons where so many doors*
> *Will open on the cold eternal shores*
> *That look sheer down*
> *To the dark tideless floods of Nothingness*
> *Where all who know may drown.*

No answer to the climactic question has been presented,
or even clearly suggested, within the poem; on the contrary, the poem leaves one with the clear impression that
science has certainly made it clear that there is nothing
after now and that all will indeed come to nought. So one
is left echoing the question, why live? It does not modify
one's impression of the poem as a poem nor clarify its
actual structure to learn that Robinson explained in a letter written shortly after its appearance that it was intended as "a protest against a material explanation of the
universe."

Since it is not my purpose here to attempt a complete
critique of the poem, I have omitted specific comment
on the verse as such. But it is not only the logical struc-

ture—or lack of it—which makes the poem a significant revelation of the effect of the cosmic chill. Consider, for example, the ending from the point of view of its language and figures. Three rhyme words are capitalized in the last eleven lines; because they are both rhyme words and capitalized, they receive the chief emphasis in the climax of the poem. They are *Nought, Now,* and *Nothingness.* Generalized diction seems to me appropriate to certain kinds of poetry, but the effect here of the vague abstractions is surely to suggest the collapse of both poetic technique and controlled feeling. Even the *Nothingness* which receives the final emphasis has not been imaginatively felt, it has only been vaguely feared. Its alternative has not even been conceived. Compare the "nothing at all" that concludes MacLeish's "End of the World," where nothingness becomes a felt quality.

Even those three figures in the last eleven lines which are not wholly abstract are highly generalized; lacking precision, the "dungeons," "cold eternal shores," and "dark tideless floods" can have only a vague emotional import. They are evidences not only that Robinson too often availed himself of worn nineteenth-century language, but also that he did not really quite know, so far as he expressed himself in this poem, what it was he feared and what it was he hoped. Such was the effect of the cosmic chill on a poet who for other reasons and other poems deserves to rank as one of the chief modern American poets.[7]

[7] It seems to me that the best case for Robinson's importance as a poet has been made by Yvor Winters in his excellent little book, *Edwin Arlington Robinson* in the New Directions Makers of Modern Literature Series (Norfolk, Conn., 1946).

4. *The Effect of the Revelations*

"The springs of philosophical thought," Susanne K. Langer has written, "have run dry once more. For fifty years at least, we have witnessed all the characteristic symptoms that mark the end of an epoch. . . . We have arrived once more at that counsel of despair, to find a reasoned faith."[8] Robinson's attempt to find such a faith was fruitless, as perhaps any such attempt, pursued in the way he pursued it, must have been. Science was the antagonist he feared; philosophy, which might have helped him to understand the significance of science as a part of man's experience and one of his ways of using his intelligence, he distrusted. For Robinson, as for the average literate man today, philosophy had become academic, unimportant, as the philosophy of the Schoolmen had become to the literate man of the Renaissance. In his published letters, there is no evidence that he profited from the revolutionary thought of Bergson and Whitehead or cared to become fully acquainted with the traditional pragmatic positivism of Dewey. True, he read Herbert Spencer with enthusiasm, Nietzsche and Schopenhauer with partial approval, and William James and Royce with disapproval during and just after his college days; yet for a philosophic poet he strikes one as rather innocent of philosophy. Like his own Miniver Cheevy, he "thought, and thought, and thought, and thought about it," but with no apparent results. "Was ever an insect flying between two flowers Told less than we are told of what we are?" He could find no starting place and he had

8 *Philosophy in a New Key: A Study in the Symbolism of Reason, Rite, and Art* (Cambridge, Mass., 1942), 13.

no method. All thinking, including the thinking involved in science, starts from unproved assumptions, but Robinson could assume nothing, not even the reality of his own experience. When he asserted that the universe "must" be purposive, he meant only that unless it is, suicide is logically called for; and he could never be sure that suicide was not called for.

In an age when the rational disciplines no longer commanded respect—his low opinions of logic and theology are cases in point—and when the implications of Newtonian science seemed to indicate that life, mind, purpose, and value were irrelevant to an estimate of the nature of reality, Robinson could not conceive that the method of observation and experiment so successfully followed by the older sciences could be right for the subject matter of those sciences without being the only valid method of inquiry in all areas. He could not conceive of any valid criticism of that "bifurcation of nature" which, as Whitehead has shown,[9] arose partly as a historical accident and partly as a response to a practical need. He felt that there must be something that science was leaving out; he did deny scientific positivism; but he could not articulate his feeling or offer grounds for his denial. He was wholly unacquainted with the thought of one of the greatest ages of reason Western culture has known, the age of Aquinas. With the proper New Englander's amused contempt for Popery, he was more inclined to

9 *Science and the Modern World* (New York, 1925). My indebtedness to all of Whitehead's work that I am capable of following without advanced mathematical training is so profound that I shall ordinarily be unable to acknowledge specific points of indebtedness, since I am no longer always aware of which of my ideas come from Whitehead and which do not.

judge the validity of Christianity by Christian Science than by Catholicism. Though he sorely missed the lost faith, though he enjoyed his own variety of religious experience, he felt in his youth that William James was no match for Herbert Spencer, and his last letters and poems suggest that he at least half agreed with John Burroughs' somewhat fatuous pronouncement that "Natural knowledge is in the ascendant. The sun of science has actually risen . . . and the things proper to the twilight or half-knowledge of a few centuries ago flee away, or are seen to be shadows and illusions."

He did not enjoy the new sunlight. He missed the shadows and wished that he were not compelled to recognize the illusions as such. "Is there a God. . . . Is there a Purpose or a Law?" he made his characters cry. But despite the urgency of his need for faith, all that he could confidently assert from within the Spencerian system was that if the world was really constituted as modern knowledge said it was, then life was not worth while. No wonder that his "religious" and "philosophic" poetry is mostly verbose, tedious, and vague. All the words, all the thinking, come to so little! Without Frost's tough-mindedness or Eliot's instinct for the nourishing elements in traditional culture, he could find no way of answering Lord Russell's rhetorical question. In the "alien and inhuman world" in which he thought he found himself, he could discover no way to keep his aspirations untarnished.

Like Hawthorne at the end of his life, he suffered from a sense of discouragement so profound that he could neither express it nor wholly repress it. Like Hawthorne's attempts in the late romances, his attempts at affirmation sound the more hollow the oftener they are repeated. Like

39

Hawthorne again, he had in early and middle life found the symbols he needed to express a sensibility still sufficiently unified to permit artistic symbolization. Like Hawthorne, finally, he shivered in a frozen world until the cosmic chill congealed the artistic powers that had once been his.

III. Robert Frost:
The Strategic Retreat

*Man is, and yet is not, involved in the flux of
nature and time. He is a creature, subject to nature's necessities and limitations; but he is also a
free spirit who knows the brevity of his years and
by this knowledge transcends the temporal by
some capacity within himself.*

—REINHOLD NIEBUHR
in The Nature and Destiny of Man

1. *Storm Fear*

Robert Frost remarked a few years ago that he was not
the "Platonist" Robinson was,[1] thus shrewdly suggesting the essential temperamental difference between
himself and the poet with whom he must always be compared. Robinson's longing for truth and meaning was
perhaps bound to be frustrated, given his time and place
and temperament; bound to be frustrated at any time or
any place, says Mr. Frost, acknowledging his "tendency
to scoff" at "literary tears" shed over man's plight. It is
easy, then, to classify Robinson as a frustrated idealist
and Frost as a satisfied, perhaps a complacent, realist,
using those terms in their popular sense; easy, and for
some purposes no doubt useful, but there are other approaches more revealing.

For Mr. Frost, too, has persistently felt and written

[1] Quoted in Lawrance Thompson, *Fire and Ice* (New York, 1942),
192.

41

about man's need for more certainty than is required for merely practical purposes. "The artist in me cries out for design," he has said;[2] yet he has not restrained his inclination to scoff. He *rejects* myth and metaphysics; the blind do not reject color. His philosophy of the limited may finally come to seem, as it has recently been fashionable to point out, a limitation in his work, but it is not a naïve philosophy. It is based on a willful, a consciously designed and elaborately guarded rejection. He has made a strategic retreat from a world with which he has acknowledged a lover's quarrel.

There is a difference, Mr. Frost has remarked, between a flight and a retreat. The one step backward that he has taken to save himself from going down with the avalanche may be characterized not as a flight but as a seeking, or it may be thought of simply as a calculated strategy. In any case it is the dominant note in the poetry from *A Boy's Will* to *A Masque of Mercy*. The note is struck in the most youthful poems. "Into My Own," the first poem in *A Boy's Will,* is both Emersonian (one goes apart to discover the true self) and Frostian in a way that Emerson would have had difficulty in understanding (one is haunted by the dark trees, one actually embraces the doom without calling it by a different name in the next sentence). The difference from the Emersonian way is crucial—partly because there is so much of Emerson in Frost. Emerson's strategy, as he admitted in *Nature,* had been to embrace idealism as a way of transforming the unpleasant facts that made the young men sad; he admitted the facts, particularly in the late *Conduct of*

2 Unless otherwise identified, all quotations from Mr. Frost are from his poetry.

Life, but his usual way was to follow the admission with a denial, or at least to change the subject quickly.

Not so the youthful Frost. His time of year is the fall, his time of day the night. He writes no poems about spring. The early poems of *A Boy's Will*—though they often betray that groping for an idiom and an attitude characteristic of youthful poetry, though they do not always have what we have come to recognize as the true Frost ring, though they are often within a tradition we have come not to admire—yet recognize the lifelong problem and suggest the lifelong answer. "My November Guest" avows "the love of bare November days." Despite its remnants of nineteenth-century poetic diction, its "o'ers," "do blow," and the like, it suggests the later Frost by announcing the presence of that neutral universe which Emerson had thought to exorcize with his "ideal theory." "Storm Fear" states the result: we must "save ourselves unaided." (Robinson had felt it impossible to save ourselves unaided; Frost called him a Platonist.) When the young poet looks, in "Vantage Point," at the homes of men, he sees, just beyond, the graves of men. "Now Close the Windows" recognizes that "it will be long ere the earliest bird." "In Hardwood Groves" urges acceptance of the world as it is, little as the heart may like it; "Reluctance" shows the heart still seeking, unwilling to accept the end of a season. During a line storm the young man thinks of "the sea's return," the ages before man, the "ancient lands," a thought that brings its own desolation. But the poet has already decided to counter hate with love, to embrace with one arm the better to strike with the other: "The fact is the sweetest dream that labor knows."

Here then in the earliest poems are the provocation

and the essence of the strategic response: a diminished world, and acceptance without approval. The situation to which acceptance without approval was the response was of course, in the largest sense, "our world" as Mr. Frost saw it. He saw it then and he sees it now as "diminished" even while he scoffs at the victims of the modern temper. What chiefly diminished it, is too clear to need further demonstration of the kind I once supplied in an earlier study of the poet.[3] There are too many direct and indirect references to science as the antagonist and too many clear statements on the matter—Mr. Frost's poetry is nearer to the poetry of statement than to symbolism—to leave anyone acquainted with the poetry in doubt. But the nature of the issue should be noted.

Man longs for reasons, ultimately for a Reason; but science, which seems to be our only dependable knowledge, gives none. And contemporary thought, taking its cue from science, denies the possibility of there being any. The old reasons, though possibly specious, kept off the dark. Like Hemingway's universal symbol of the old man who wanted to stay in a clean, well-lighted place, Frost has yearned for light. But what the heart demands, the mind, in our time, cannot supply. Science has given us light of a kind, but it has taken away the light we most desire, leaving us only a "flickering, human pathetic light" that we strive to "maintain against the night." Time and space have been enlarged until we are diminished into nothing. (So that we are in the same plight as the men of the Middle Ages, who were dwarfed by God; all ages are the same for the soul.[4]) "Space ails us

3 In *American Literature,* Vol. XIII, No. 3 (November, 1941), 207–23.
4 See "The Lesson for Today."

moderns: we are sick with space." We have "taken artificial light Against the ancient sovereignty of night," but it is not bright enough to keep us unaware of "the heartless and enormous Outer Black." The literate farmer argued that science "cheapened speed," but the poet replied that "A good cheap anti-dark is now the need." In our day science holds "the ministry of fear"; our science "unnerves" us:

> *He thought if he could have his space all curved . . . .*
> *His science wouldn't get him so unnerved.*

The darkness is complete, being both interstellar and philosophic: as Job said to God in *A Masque of Reason,*

> *We don't know where we are, or who we are*
> *Don't know one another; don't know You;*
> *Don't know what time it is . . . .*
> *It comes down to a doubt about the wisdom*
> *Of having children—after having had them.*

As science brings more light of fact, it increases the darkness of the understanding. It looked to the young Frost, as it looks to him now, as if

> *. . . a night of dark intent*
> *Was coming, and not only a night, an age.*

2. *The Response*

The heart of man is terrified by the dark, but his mind can do something—not enough, but something—to discipline the heart. What I have called Frost's strategy is precisely the response of the mind to a situation at which the heart rebels. From the earliest to the latest poems

45

we may observe the maneuver developing until it becomes the poet's characteristic stance.

North of Boston, the poet's second volume, is made up almost entirely of long narrative and dramatic poems on New England characters, but when the poet returned, in *Mountain Interval,* to the lyric, he returned to the theme which had been present only as a mood in the character studies. "Oven Bird" determines the key of *Mountain Interval;* it phrases the crucial question: the question is "what to make of a diminished thing." Both "Hyla Brook" and "In the Home Stretch" suggest the elements of an answer: there are no ends and beginnings, only middles; don't remember too much, don't look too far; "We love the things we love for what they are." And "The Exposed Nest" and "Out, Out—" further emphasize the attitude: the way to take the diminished thing is not to care too much, to turn back to one's affairs.

New Hampshire, the fourth volume, continues the strain with increased emphasis. Many of the poems develop the theme of the limitation of man's knowledge. "Some may know what they seek in school and church," but the poet is content to hold in his hand the meteoric fragment which is, he feels, "the one world . . . I am like to compass." The certainty man would like to pin his faith to has been sought in vain: "We've looked and looked, but after all where are we?" Using the figure of the telescope, "The Star Splitter" humorously and "I Will Sing You One O" seriously deny the usefulness of science in man's quest for certainty. Fragmentary blue must suffice those for whom a view of Heaven has become impossible. Now and then clear days come even in New England to whet our desire for a more perfect blue, but one had best not count on them. Once truth seemed to glimmer as a pebble at the bottom of a well, then something . . . . The poet hopes he will go after the knowledge "beyond the bounds of life" when he is free to. Meanwhile, there is a life to live and the way to live it is not to cling too tightly, to learn to let go with the mind ("Wild Grapes"), to accept the end of a season ("Nothing Gold Can Stay"), to learn that the phoebes are not weeping for the burned house on the deserted farm ("The Need of Being Versed in Country Things").

West Running Brook saw the poet at the height of his powers, and several of the finest lyrics in the volume are on the theme which it is my present concern to trace. "Once by the Pacific" foresees a dark night ahead for the soul. "The Peaceful Shepherd" suggests a willingness to forget the crown, the scales, and the cross, since we may know them by their fruits. "A Winter Eden" offers us the only kind of Eden we are likely to know; we had better make the most of it, though

> *An hour of winter day might seem too short*
> *To make it worth life's while to wake and sport.*

And in one of the loveliest lyrics in all his verse the poet insists on what should have been clear to everyone, though it has not been to those who have thought of his strategy as a flight from "reality": "I have been one acquainted with the night."

Two poems in *West Running Brook* state afresh the reason for the strategy. When he looks up by chance at the constellations, the poet is reminded that there is no revelation in nature; and in "The Bear" he expounds humorously on man's pathetic attempts to reach cer-

47

tainty: like a caged bear, man seeks restlessly in science and philosophy for the absolutes which neither can provide; neither telescope nor microscope, Plato nor Aristotle can answer the questions we most want answered. In Emersonian fashion the poem scoffs at the claims of reason, but its failure to mention the alternative of intuition marks the poet's difference from the master. Man simply goes on swaying futilely back and forth from cheek to cheek—that is, when he is not pacing with equal futility back and forth from telescope to microscope and back to telescope. "All revelation" may have been ours, as the poet says in a later poem, but it is not the kind we seem to know how to use. It is discernible anyway only to those whose eyes are turned in the right direction, only, in short, to those who have mastered the defensive strategy.

An ever increasing proportion of the poems in the later volumes, especially in *A Further Range, A Witness Tree,* and *Steeple Bush,* reiterate and amplify the complex of attitudes which I have been tracing. Several of the poems devoted to it—"Desert Places" and "Come In," for example—are among the very finest the poet has ever written. But without commenting further on individual poems, I want to summarize the several aspects of the challenge and the strategic response and turn to their final significance in all of the poetry.

The dark, the doom, the not knowing can be accepted by the mind, but the heart rebels. When the light flickers and the gloom increases, the mind takes a quick step back to "common sense," to "matter of fact," and continues to accept a life that sometimes looks "sinister-grave." The mind accepts time's tearing down what has been built up, the inhuman perspectives of geology and astronomy, the loneliness and cold of "the long night." The mind counters the heart's fear by suggesting that "it's knowing what to do with things that counts." Though man can see neither out far nor in deep, and though his attempts to interpret his most certain knowledge result only in a futile turning "from force to matter and back to force," yet man has his defenses:

> *The Infinite's being so wide*
> *Is the reason the Powers provide*
> *For my inner defense my hide.*

With defenses intact—and mental as well as biological forces have contrived them—the poet can afford to stand "freely face to face All night with universal space." He can feel the loneliness that comes on in desert places (a loneliness that "will be more lonely ere it will be less"), recognize that the stars have "no expression, nothing to express," yet remain unfrightened. He has learned not to care when he tramples the autumn leaves in the mud, thus hastening the end of a season; and if he even takes a sort of pleasure in the trampling, perhaps it is because fear sometimes makes us destroy what we love.

> *Perhaps I have put forth too much strength and*
> *   been too fierce from fear.*
> *I have safely trodden underfoot the leaves of*
> *   another year.*

The poet long ago decided that the "discipline man needed most Was to learn submission to unreason." He has adopted an attitude of pragmatic acquiescence, a variety of positivism that would suggest the position of the logical positivists, were it not that the poet's laughter is directed at science even more often than it is at meta-physics. Having achieved his difficult renunciation, Mr. Frost is able in his poetry to practice what Mr. Eliot has hoped to learn: "to care and not to care." The achieve-ment has been the result of the unremitting effort of a lifetime. To trace this effort is to realize how accurate the poet is when he says in a late poem:

> *I have been so instinctively thorough*
> *About my crevice and burrow.*

3. *Denials and Affirmations*

Mr. Frost is a man of many denials. His personal manner, his conservative political position, the harshness with which he usually judges his contemporaries—these and more aspects of a cultivated hardness need not concern us here. But his denials, as we have already seen, are not limited to things political, social, and personal, nor do they all set him off from his time. On the contrary, his denial of the value of systematic reason is quite in keep-ing with the temper of an age which fears the tyranny of words and has ceased studying philosophy. And his denial of the value of theology,[5] side by side with his ac-ceptance of the religious spirit as a natural part of man, strikes a purely contemporary, though not an advanced contemporary, note. Only men go in for metaphysics and theology; "You don't catch women trying to be Plato."

[5] By which I mean the rational clarification and systematization of religious doctrines, insights, or revelations, but by which the general pub-lic today—including, it would seem, Mr. Frost—means the rationalization of superstition, an activity at best useless and at worst pernicious. See *A Masque of Reason*, "The Fear of God," "Innate Helium," "Skeptic," and "Etherealizing."

In his humorous and inconclusive poem on the problem of evil, the poet treats Job's wife more sympathetically than he does Job, just as in some of the early character studies, he showed more sympathy for the women than for the men. Women have never been much concerned with Truth "in the abstract high singular."

But it is chiefly the two denials that he makes with regard to science that concern us here. First, what science reveals is neither so new nor so important as its more excited devotees suppose. The "sun of science" may actually have risen, as John Burroughs put it, but the shadows have not receded and the day is not perceptibly different in the ways that count most. "The truths we keep coming back and back to" are still with us, and though "thought cleaves the interstellar gloom," it is not to admit any light that much alters our condition. In psychology as in the other sciences, what is taken to be completely new is frequently as old as the Greeks:

> *The already known had once more been confirmed*
> *By psychological experiment.*[6]

News of the expanding universe is usually referred to humorously in the poems: "The world's size has no more to do with us Than has the universe's." In short, whatever the Truth may be, whatever the nature of the Secret that "sits in the middle and knows, While we dance round in a ring and suppose," at least the poet "will not have it systematic."

---

[6] A more striking illustration of this attitude was Mr. Frost's contention, in a conversation with me some years ago, that the essence of Einsteinian relativity, all that is philosophically important in the theory, is contained in Emerson's "Uriel." See my article in *American Literature* cited in n. 3 above.

Second, Mr. Frost has denied as firmly as ever Hawthorne or Thoreau did that science will usher in a
Utopia. "Science ought to know," of course, since it
knows everything else, but the millenium which is so
near now ("It is almost the year 2000"), this "end de
luxe" promised us, seems more likely to be a "bursting
rapture" provided by atomic physics than what the devotees of "scientism" have imagined. As life comes to be
more and more dominated by science, pure and applied
("But now 'twas there as elsewhere, any gain Was made
by getting science on the brain"), it becomes increasingly
questionable whether or not the change should be called
"progress." "Scientism" is Mr. Frost's word for an uncritical attitude toward science, and it says all that needs
to be said on the subject.

Balancing these denials are three major affirmations
in Mr. Frost's poetry. There is, first, faith in the pragmatic intelligence. Because we have intelligence,

> We will not be put off the final goal
> We have it hidden in us to attain.

The tree fallen across the road only stimulates our in-
genuity; we will find a way around. The world was obviously not planned for man's convenience or comfort,
but, though nature often appears to be actively hostile,

> She may know cove and cape,
> But she does not know mankind
> If by any change of shape,
> She hopes to cut off mind.

Of the many expressions of faith in the pragmatic intelligence, perhaps "Riders" is the most memorable. "What is this talked of mystery of birth But being mounted bareback on the earth?"

> *The surest thing there is is we are riders*
> *And though none too successful at it, guiders,*
> *Through everything presented, land and tide*
> *And now the very air, of what we ride.*

The intelligence that is helpless to find answers to ultimate questions is not easily thwarted in practical affairs: "We have ideas yet we haven't tried."

The second affirmation is everywhere in the poems implied, and perhaps less frequently stated than the first only because it is so basic and, to the poet, so obvious: it is the right of the individual to go his own way. The presence in Mr. Frost's work of a kind of individualism very like Emerson's has several times been commented on and need not be stressed here. Like the author of "Uriel," which in *A Masque of Reason* he called "the greatest Western poem yet," Mr. Frost bids us to "a one-man revolution" and warns that we're "too unseparate." "Steal away and steal away. Don't join too many gangs."

The third affirmation completes the other two and is the necessary logical basis of the mood of acceptance that the poet has been able to protect by staying close to his strategic burrow. I think it can most accurately be called a recognition of the naturalness of life and mind. Surely it is neither "optimism" nor religious faith in any ordinary sense, as so many of the poet's critics would have it. Lawrance Thompson, in his book on the poetry, has written that "Sitting by a Bush" is "motivated by a strong religious faith," yet what the poem asserts is only that what is called elsewhere the "innate helium" of the religious spirit is as native to us as our breath; the *fact* of life is the basis of our faith. Though this poem comes closer than any other to supplying an argument for those who want to believe that the poet is some sort of Christian, it does not come even as close to the historic faith as the vaguest sort of Protestant modernism, which the poet has blasted in *A Masque of Reason* in the *tendency* passage. True, the contrast between Watsonian behaviorism and other forms of materialism in our day, on the one hand, and Mr. Frost's recognition of the reality and even the "natural-ness" of life and mind, on the other, makes it possible to apply the term "idealistic" to the poet's outlook; but the difference between that outlook and the outlook of any historic religion is so great that to call any of the poems re-ligious without a preliminary definition of terms can only lead to confusion. If we are to be clear about what "Sitting by a Bush," for instance, asserts, we can only return to the poem itself and insist that it be attended to: life began "When dust really took in the sun" and religious faith began with it—both, it is implied, being natural products of the earth's processes. This is more nearly the assertion of a fact, or what is taken to be a fact, than of a faith.

A fuller statement of the same attitude is found in "West Running Brook." Beginning and ending as it does with the brook itself, the downward flow which suggests the degradation of energy, science's second law of thermo-dynamics, it asserts the *naturalness* of the eddy which the current flings back upon itself. The ripple seems to be defying the current, but a hidden rock explains it. Mov-ing ever upward against the stream, it is analogous to life maintaining itself in

The universal cataract of death
That spends to nothingness—and unresisted,
Save by some strange resistance in itself . . . .
Our life runs down in sending up the clock.
The brook runs down in sending up our life.
The sun runs down in sending up the brook.
And there is something sending up the sun.
It is this backward motion toward the source,
Against the stream, that most we see ourselves in,
It is from this in nature we are from.

We have here of course a figure comparable to Bergson's fountain, though significantly in Frost's poem the downward rush creates the ripple while in Bergson's metaphor the upward surge, the *élan vital,* is the primary force. Although it is possible to acknowledge the likeness between Frost and Bergson that Mr. Thompson points out,[7] what seems to me more prominent and significant is the difference between the outlooks of the two. Mr. Frost's ideas are not apt ever to serve as the cornerstone of any church.[8]

Just how irrelevant to the religious attitude and religious needs Mr. Frost's outlook finally is when traced to its most general expression may be better suggested by his often implied, occasionally asserted faith that the universe is somewhat more for us than against, else "our hold on the planet wouldn't have so increased." This is, of course, a denial of some of the more extreme of the conclusions sometimes drawn from the "alien universe" concept, a denial that life is a "disease of matter," that man is a doomed biological accident. Yet the denial of

[7] *Fire and Ice,* 197.
[8] See T. S. Eliot, *The Rock* (New York, 1934), 22.

such ideas as these does not in itself make one religious, and one may hold such ideas and be in a manner religious, as we shall see in the case of Robinson Jeffers. To say that the universe is more for us than against us is simply to assert a naturalism that includes biology rather than one which is based exclusively on physics. Religions are not built on such affirmations as this.

4. *The Craft as Expression*

The strategic retreat is as apparent in Mr. Frost's idiom as it is in the attitudes expressed in his poems. The symbols most characteristic of his poetry, commonly drawn from country sights and sounds, are symbols of diminution, of deprivation, of retreat and acceptance. The closing of the windows, the falling of the leaves, the unmelodious late-summer song of the ovenbird, darkness, cold, the flickering light, the deserted house, the abandoned farm, the lost opportunity, the steeple bush which marks the end of a pasture's usefulness for farming, the backward step to avoid disaster, storm fear and home burial, bare trees, the sweet beckoning call of the hermit thrush in the dark evergreen woods at evening—these are the stuff of the poems. Anyone who should care to count and classify all the symbols in Mr. Frost's poems would find, I think, that a significant majority of them are the ones I have named or their like, and that they convey a mood of disciplined acceptance. Like Joseph Conrad's major symbol in "The Heart of Darkness," the poet's darkness is that of a naturalist whose heart rebels at the ring of iron but whose mind is occupied in trying to make the situation acceptable. (It is significant, however, that the poet's use of darkness parallels only two of the levels of meaning of the symbol in Conrad's story, the level suggested by Marlowe's reference to "jewels flashing in the night of time" and that suggested by the jungle. Conrad's story seems to me far more complex than any Frost poem.) Notable, too, is the number of times the poet draws on the concepts, terminology, and facts of science, especially of astronomy and geology, for his figures, almost always with one of two effects: either to suggest the nature of "the heartless and enormous outer black" or to disparage, humorously, those who take science so seriously as either to pin all their hopes on it or to be utterly distressed by it. In short, the poet's favorite symbols are as eloquent as is a prose paraphrase of his poems of an attitude of reluctant acceptance of a diminished world.

So, too, his characteristic devices of understatement, humor, and plainness. When understatement is not simply a device for humor, it is a guarded way of saying things, a way characteristic not only of Yankees but of anyone who does not wish to feel or say too much. Mr. Frost is chiefly a lyric poet, but like the ovenbird which he has honored, he has been able to continue singing long after others have ceased because he knows "in singing not to sing." Understatement, interestingly enough one of the favorite literary devices of our day, is as much a defensive gesture in Mr. Frost's work as it is in that of Ernest Hemingway.

Humor is Mr. Frost's way of taking an unpleasant reality. He has noted that there are only two ways to take the world, "tragic or comic." His humor is as much a reaction to perceived tragedy as are the "literary tears," as he calls them, of different temperaments, of, say, a Robinson or an Eliot. If his acknowledged tendency to scoff makes him seem at times insensitive, we should not be misled by it into thinking that he is at heart simply a jolly fellow or that the intention of his poems is to be funny. Though some poems like "Departmental" exist chiefly as poetic jokes, the great bulk of the poetry exhibits humor functioning as a conscious thickening of the skin, a careful strengthening of the "inner defense."

The plainness of speech in Mr. Frost's poems, like his unlaced tennis shoes and his rumpled hair, is not only an expression of his personality—and all mature personalities are in part consciously contrived, are, in no pejorative sense, poses, maneuvers, strategies, masks—it is also a stylistic expression of the conviction that "the fact is the sweetest dream that labor knows." Earlier, more illusioned poets tended to transform or transcend facts, to heighten style, to aspire to the sublime. Mr. Frost prefers the horizontal analogy and the low-pressure, conversational phrase. That his early experiments in this type of poetry constituted one of the most significant poetic advances of the early twentieth century does not in any way diminish the pertinence of the observation that his special way of saying things is in the nature of a retreat both from a too florid, and so defenseless, poetry and from a too trusting, and so likewise defenseless, view of the world.

5. *"The Armful"*

If Robert Frost has refused to "come in" to the dark which he has so constantly and clearly perceived, it is not because he has perceived without understanding, but because he has preferred the way of hardening himself to an unpleasant reality to that of either succumbing to it or, as he would have it, deluding himself about it. One of the most perfect symbols to suggest his whole strategy may be found in "The Armful." Trying to carry many ill-assorted parcels, trying to keep them all somehow precariously in balance, but realizing that despite his best efforts some will fall, the poet *stoops* to prevent the fall— and *prevent* is used in the poem in the older sense of *to anticipate*. The strategy has been to try to anticipate the inevitable. If such a policy entails a stooping posture, it likewise lessens the destruction of life's various and conflicting values. So, too, Emerson, with his ambiguous dualistic monism, his spontaneity of fate, and his deification of the whole course of things, tried to soften the fall from Christian supernaturalism to scientific naturalism. Mr. Frost's position is, in many more respects than I have found it possible to mention, basically Emersonian. Like Emerson's, it is the result of the effort of a sturdy and cheerful temperament to adjust itself to an unpleasantly changed reality.

But it is the modifications which Mr. Frost has made in Emersonianism, modifications forced by his perception of a "stormy stormy world," rather than the Emersonianism itself, which are interesting. Endeavoring not to be "resentful of man's condition," he has followed a different path from that of Robinson, in whom also one may discern Emersonian elements. Unlike Robinson, who thought life not worth while if man were deprived of the Light, he has made what light he has do; and unlike Mr. Eliot, who has refused to stoop to prevent the dropping of values, who has gladly dropped a great many values indeed the better to cling to the highest, he has balanced the load and tightened his grip. Adopting the dusk as his special time of day as morning was Thoreau's, he has been able to say that, as gloom was wasted on a character in one of his poems, so

> *It is on me by night or day,*
> *Who have, as I suppose, ahead*
> *The darkest of it still to dread.*

Mr. Frost has saved himself from Robinson's melancholy, Eliot's pious despair, and Crane's agony by not asking for a Purpose or a Law, by not attempting to redeem or regenerate the natural, by not listening for the sounding heel of Elohim, by cracking a joke and listening instead for an ovenbird; in short, by accepting a diminished thing. His strategic retreat has prevented both conquest and rout, as planned retreats are apt to do. His grand maneuver is his answer to Lord Russell's question, "How, in such an alien and inhuman world, can so powerless a creature as Man preserve his aspirations untarnished?"

IV. T. S. Eliot: at the Still Point

*Western Christendom may be given grace to be
born again as a* Respublica Christiana, *which was
its own earlier and better ideal of what it should
strive to be.*
—ARNOLD TOYNBEE *in* A Study of History.

1. *Three Ways*

The study of history is an art and a branch of philosophy as well as, in a very limited sense, a science. The revelations it affords us spring from our assumptions and are called forth by our questions. Yet the sense of occasional revelation remains and may not be wholly illusion.

The year 1925 provides a suggestive configuration. In that year three books, each the outstanding publication of the year in its field, date the end of a tradition and two different kinds of a beginning. Theodore Dreiser's *An American Tragedy,* his best and most famous novel, marked the end of fictional materialistic naturalism in the tradition of Zola, and Alfred North Whitehead's *Science and the Modern World* and T. S. Eliot's *The Hollow Men* mark the two beginnings. The generation of materialism found belatedly its fullest expression in the novel, and the new age whose shape we cannot yet wholly discern found its beginnings in the philosopher and the poet.

If James T. Farrell carries on the Dreiser tradition in increasingly unreadable and unread novels, and if

Bergson had anticipated Whitehead and Eliot in his earlier poetry had anticipated *The Hollow Men,* the case for 1925's being a pivotal date is not completely demolished: for I do not know of any other year in which the three chief works in fiction, philosophy, and poetry throw, separately and in conjunction, so clear and far-reaching a light on the issues of our time. Dreiser wept over the fate imposed on man by "chemisms" in a world of nothing real but matter and motion. Whitehead revised our picture of the world in such a way as to give status to life and mind. And Mr. Eliot completed the exposure of the men made hollow by scientific secularism begun in *The Waste Land* and continued his quest of the still point in the dream-crossed twilight between birth and dying. All the portents, all the possibilities even, of our age are here: from H. L. Mencken to Kafka and Kierkegaard as college-cult heroes; the turning to Christian or mystical faith of the best British writers of the generation who were in college when Dreiser was idolized; the startling contrast between the most prominent philosopher of history of the twenties and the one who has made the greatest impact on the forties, between Spengler and Toynbee, materialist and Christian historians; the countless popular books of the last fifteen years urging a "return to religion" and a "rediscovery of man"; the increasing influence outside of conservative churches of Reinhold Niebuhr (Before Niebuhr, how far back do we have to go to find a theologian influential in American intellectual circles?); the increasing number of Thomists in places of influence; the eclipse of Watsonian behaviorism (which psychologists now like to say no one ever took seriously, but which dominated American college teaching of psychology for

at least a decade and which is still not dead among semanticists and many varieties of pseudo-scientists); the rise
of *Gestalt* and the revisions and excisions made by the
eclectic Freudians and the analysts of the Horney and
Fromm schools; charges of a failure of nerve from the
Deweyite positivists and overstated counterclaims for the
consequences which ideas have—all these aspects of the
intellectual ferment of our seemingly transitional age are
here suggested in three books.

The issues are here and the alternative possibilities:
continuation of the naturalism based on naïve materialism which for several centuries had been revealing with
ever increasing clarity that life, mind, and value were accidental or even illusory in the world of matter and motion which it found real; radical modification of naturalism along lines suggested by the sciences of life rather
than those of the inanimate; or rejection of the whole
naturalist tradition in favor of supernaturalism. Of the
first two ways I shall say nothing more here, though they
are still very much with us. Mr. Eliot's way, the rejection
of the dominant trends of thought and social change since
the Renaissance, is my subject.

2. *Philosophy as Preparation*

Philip Wheelwright has remarked,[1] rightly I think, that
there are for Mr. Eliot two chief modes of apprehension,
the poetic and the religious. Yvor Winters has shown,[2]

[1] "Eliot's Philosophical Themes," in *T. S. Eliot, Focus Three,* edited
by B. Rajan (London, 1947).
[2] "T. S. Eliot: The Illusion of Reaction," in *In Defense of Reason*
(New York, 1947).

in an essay that includes some distortion and overemphasis and exhibits its author's usual blind spots but that succeeds in making its basic point, that Mr. Eliot is not a logical critic, that there is much confusion in the implications of his unstated critical system. Many have remarked the offhand, inconsecutive, and unsupported, the *ex cathedra,* nature of Mr. Eliot's pronouncements on large and difficult matters. And the poet's comments in his prose on philosophers and philosophy are few, casual, and largely on matters other than the strictly philosophical—on the style and charm of certain philosophers, for instance.

Yet if all this seems odd in one who once studied for the doctorate in philosophy at Harvard and abroad, a moment's reflection enables one to see it as part of a larger pattern. For, quite apart from matters of temperament, the poet's conscious reaction against modern secular culture has been so complete that it includes all the philosophy that prefigured and, to an unknown extent, shaped that culture. Hence the former student of philosophy cites Heraclitus and Krishna, the Bible and the mystics and the theologians, but scarcely mentions except casually any Western philosopher since Descartes. Hence the poet who once worked on a dissertation on F. H. Bradley, the poet who, I should judge, is better acquainted with the chief philosophers than any other of the poets we are considering, seems less philosophical in any obvious sense than any important modern English or American poet with the exception of Wallace Stevens. Mr. Eliot knows the tradition of philosophy from Descartes to Dewey and he does not approve. His strategy is not to argue but to ignore.

But there are modern philosophers to whom Mr. Eliot is indebted or to whose ideas his own have a close relationship; there is even a minor tradition of which he partially approves. Since that part of this tradition which bears on the problems of science and religion is the part on which Mr. Eliot and his critics have had least to say, I should like to do something to supply the lack, for the poet did not begin as a follower of the mystics or discover in infancy the folly of trusting to science. What he has called his "intellectual assent" to orthodoxy has roots in a stream of modern thought which, if one is acquainted with it, makes his conversion seem something less than miraculous. So without attempting at all to distinguish all the influences to which Mr. Eliot has been subject, without examining the development of his poetic theory, a topic which has been well treated by Mr. Matthiessen in his book on the poet, I should like to touch upon certain aspects of the ideas of several of the thinkers to whom Mr. Eliot has acknowledged indebtedness or with whom he has indicated his agreement. I do not know all the books which may have influenced Mr. Eliot; I do know that his attitude toward science and related problems of philosophy and religion is foreshadowed in the works of F. H. Bradley, Henri Bergson, T. E. Hulme, and Irving Babbitt.

In the essay on Bradley in which in 1926 he paid his only full-length tribute to a philosopher, Mr. Eliot praised chiefly Bradley's early *Ethical Studies* and *Principles of Logic,* paying scant attention to the philosophy which Bradley expounded in the book for which he is remembered today, *Appearance and Reality.* It is not to be wondered at that Mr. Eliot was chiefly interested in

Bradley's style, his personality, and his ethical perception, for by 1926 the poet had fully matured his convictions and he must have found the philosophy itself obvious where it was not mistaken or irrelevant. Yet there are interesting connections between Bradley's thought and the minor tradition which has influenced the poet.

Perhaps the most important thing which Mr. Eliot did not mention in his essay is Bradley's analysis of science as abstraction. No doubt to Mr. Eliot this contribution of Bradley's seemed, in the middle twenties, too elementary to deserve attention. But historically Bradley's belief that the system of nature constructed by physical science was a "necessary working fiction" only was an important step in the direction not only of Bergson and Whitehead but of the logical positivists as well.

According to Bradley's analysis, since generally recognized as valid,[3] the very foundation of science is the process of rigid exclusion, or abstraction from a complex reality of the relatively simple facts to be studied. Thus traditional physics, for example, distinguishes primary from secondary qualities, locating the former outside and the latter inside our heads, simplifying the nature it studies by eliminating from "objective reality" all the qualitative aspects of experience. The result is nature con-

---

[3] It is recognized, I believe, not only by philosophers but by those scientists who have any philosophical understanding of what they are about. For example, A. E. Heath says in "Philosophy and Contemporary Science," in *Science for a New World* (London and New York, 1934), "Everyone now recognizes how all-pervading the act of selection is in scientific work. The scientist chooses his facts; he selects from a range of possible laws; he picks out the hypotheses which best conform to the body of his more generalized theories; and finally he comes to realize that there has been an element of choice in his general theory-systems determined by his ideals of explanation."

ceived of as matter in motion, something no one ever experienced, yet somehow the only truly *real* world; on which Bradley's sufficient comment was that

> It is doubtless scientific to disregard certain aspects when we work: but to urge that therefore such aspects are not fact, and that what we use without regard to them is an independent real thing,—this is barbarous metaphysics.

Science, then, is practical knowledge, or, as Lord Russell was later to define it, power knowledge.[4] But there is also philosophy, which aims at understanding, not control. The only way we can approach full understanding, Bradley insisted, is through a consideration of the fullness of experience. Logical thought is primarily a tool to help us to attain self-consistency, but we shall never attain entire consistency. After thought has done all it can, it remains for direct awareness, the immediacy of feeling, to tell us as much as we shall ever know of the nature of reality. All that we find in immediate experience must be attributes of nature, feeling as well as extension, color as well as mass. The dead world of kinetic atomic physics is by no means the real world, though it is an element in, an abstraction from, the total reality.

So bare a summary does not, of course, do justice to the subtle philosophy of this man who has been considered the most penetrating philosopher of his day; but it is perhaps sufficient to indicate the relationship between Bradley and Bergson, whose philosophy Mr. Eliot has alluded to in *The Rock* and whose style he has praised elsewhere. If Bradley's system offered Mr. Eliot a precedent for condemning the "barbarous metaphysics" of sci-

4 See *The Scientific Outlook* (New York, 1931), 81–84.

entism, Bergson's did more: it established intuition, religious or otherwise, as superior to scientific reasoning of any sort, no matter how civilized and self-critical.

Bergson's ideas are so generally well known that they do not need summary here, but it may be well to emphasize certain doctrines that help to define his relation to Mr. Eliot's poetry. Starting with what seemed to him the data of consciousness rather than with the traditional distinctions between subject and object and matter and mind, Bergson found the fundamental fact of experience to be its *flowing* quality. Change, not permanence, is the primary datum of consciousness. (Only the saints find the still point, says Mr. Eliot.) And the irreversible flow of consciousness is the only means we have of approaching the "real"; past and future are contained in the present, and the "matter" and "motion" and other categories of science and the logical intellect are but fumbling abstractions produced by what is essentially a tool for survival. To analyze and to argue are to distort. Although the content of consciousness lends itself to "inexhaustible enumeration," the essence of consciousness, and so of any reality we can ever know, can be grasped only by "indivisible apprehension."

On the basis of such an epistemological approach, Bergson constructed a dualistic system. There are, he thought, two tendencies in the world, an upward and a downward. Neither the experience of the individual nor our knowledge of the whole course of organic evolution can be explained as the passive product or the accidental by-product of the random action of matter in motion, as the mechanists would have it. The materialism which some have thought to be Charles Darwin's real contribution to the progress of evolutionary thought[5] is as inadequate to explain the upward surge of life, Bergson believed (as Samuel Butler had believed before him), as mechanistic psychology is to explain totally the sane and mature individual. Against the downward tendency of matter, the falling of the water in the fountain after its upward force is spent, the second law of thermodynamics in physics, against this degradation and dispersal of things life pushes upward, using the logical intellect as a tool to help it combat the inertia, the limitations, the determinateness of matter. There is a vital force in nature which science leaves out of account but which must be included in any account of reality. (Mr. Eliot has included it and given it attributes and a name.)

T. E. Hulme associated with Mr. Eliot's friend Ezra Pound in London before World War I. An early imagist and unsystematic thinker who anticipated the more recently fashionable rejection of modernism, liberalism, and especially of the nineteenth century and all its works, he seems to have influenced many men more gifted than himself. Mr. Matthiessen tells us that Eliot had developed his poetic theory before reading Hulme's *Speculations,* published posthumously, or meeting the man; yet, as Matthiessen points out,[6] there are such striking parallels between Hulme's thought and Eliot's that they are worth citing. (Matthiessen has also judged that one of Eliot's "demonstrably enduring debts" is to Hulme.) But whether Hulme's ideas constitute an influence or merely a parallel is not crucial: Hulme is an important link in

[5] An interesting expression of this point of view is to be found in Jacques Barzun's *Darwin, Marx, Wagner* (New York, 1941).

[6] In *The Achievement of T. S. Eliot* (New York, 1947), 70–71; cf. 33.

that chain, the whole length of which forms part of the poet's intellectual background.

Hulme's connection with Bergson was one of acknowledged indebtedness. In 1913 he translated Bergson's *Introduction to Metaphysics,* and had he not been killed in the war, he might have carried out his plan to write a general introduction to the master's philosophy. Yet the changes which Hulme made in Bergson's doctrines are noteworthy, suggestive as they are of the use which he was making of that philosophy.

The dualism which Bergson had observed between matter and life Hulme expanded into pluralism. There are, he asserted, three realms of reality, or, better, three distinct realities—the inorganic, the organic, and the ethical and religious. Of these three realities he frequently repeated, "There must be an *absolute* division between each of the three regions, a kind of *chasm.* There must be no continuity, no bridge leading from one to the other."[7] But though there are no connections between them, we have exact knowledge—"absolute," Hulme called it—about two of these areas, the inorganic and the ethical-religious. Thus physics and religion are equal and final authorities which can never be in conflict. That we are at this point very far indeed from both the letter and the spirit of Bergson's philosophy is obvious. It would seem that Hulme's veneration for Bergson was based on the latter's having "disproved" materialism.

Further perusal of *Speculations* strengthens one's suspicion that for Hulme, Bergson was chiefly a stepping-stone to absolutism of a sort at once political and religious. Taught by Bergson's critique of the habits of the logical

[7] *Speculations* (New York, 1924), 6.

intellect to distrust reason as it operated in philosophy—
though not, significantly, as it appeared in theology—
Hulme planned to write a "critique of satisfaction" which
would demonstrate that philosophy since the Renaissance
had been simply wishful thinking and which would dis-
pose of those "bastard phenomena . . . Romanticism in
literature, Relativism in ethics, Idealism in philosophy,
and Modernism in religion."[8] When, having indicated
that relativism in ethics must be disposed of, Hulme stated
his own ethical views, the "virtue" which he espoused
most enthusiastically was, not too surprisingly, violence.
Not content merely to aid in the spreading of the new ethics by translating Sorel's *Reflections on Violence* (which
influenced Mussolini in his formation of the doctrine of
fascism), he adopted militarism as a personal creed and
acted upon his belief by enlisting in the war in which
he was, appropriately, killed. Reacting against the romantic doctrine of the goodness of the natural man, he
discovered that the doctrine of original sin was a truer
expression of the facts of experience; but to this rediscovered Christian doctrine he added another that, like
his adoption of violence as a way of life, links him with
the growing fascist movement rather than with Christianity: he believed that only political absolutism which
would supply discipline without regard for the absurd
"romantic" reverence for the individual would enable
man to accomplish anything. Ezra Pound was not the only
potential fascist in London before World War I.

Of one other writer Mr. Eliot has said more to indi-

[8] *Ibid.*, 10. For a discussion of the parallels between scientific ideas
of discontinuity and Hulme's doctrines, see J. G. Crowther, *The Social
Relations of Science* (New York, 1941), 593–99.

cate a close relationship than he has of Bradley, Bergson, or Hulme: he has acknowledged that he began as a disciple of Irving Babbitt. Though he quickly moved beyond the type of humanism Babbitt represented and only a few years after the beginning of his voluntary exile agreed with Hulme's dictum that "It is necessary to recognize that there is an absolute, and not a relative, difference between humanism . . . and the religious spirit," yet the fundamental similarity between the outlooks of Babbitt and Eliot did not cease with the latter's discovery of the necessity of religious dogmas, as the poet himself acknowledged by saying that Babbitt was "fundamentally on most questions in the right." Nor, in saying this, need the poet have been thinking chiefly of his teacher's rejection of Rousseau and romanticism. For both men reacted early against all that the "generation of materialism" had stood for. Deeper than Babbitt's cult of refinement, deeper than his aristocratic distaste for democracy, lay his reaction against scientism. To that extent he and Eliot stand together with Robinson and Frost, unlike in most respects as these four are. As for the relationship between Babbitt and Eliot, it is perfectly clear: they start from the same place, the one as leader and the other as follower, rejecting romanticism, liberalism, democracy, and scientism; the one ends by relying on the "inner check," the other on the external authority of the church.

In short, Eliot's early following of Babbitt, his study of Bradley, and his acquaintance with the ideas of Bergson and Hulme prepared the way for his famous 1927 statement of his royalism, classicism, and Anglo-Catholicism. Bradley's reinstatement of value in the world of nature, Bergson's criticism of the notion that only science can tell us anything of reality, Hulme's diagnosis of the incompleteness of humanism (which Eliot has quoted with approval and accepted as his own), Babbitt's genteel protestations against naturalism—all these must be taken into account in any attempt to relate Mr. Eliot's poetry to its intellectual background.

3. *Science Condemned and Used*

It is customary in certain highly respected circles today to apologize for offering any discussion at all of a poet's ideas. By several of those who have had the temerity to discuss the ideas of Mr. Eliot as they are found in his poetry, we are reminded that explication of the prose meaning of the symbols or of the recurrent themes of poetry can be no more than a scaffolding tacked to the house or a map of the country. Granted. But scaffoldings and maps are often essential. To deny their usefulness is ultimately to deny that poetry has any important connection with man's conceptual activity. This extreme position I wish here to deny explicitly as my method has thus far denied it implicitly. Although some poetry is more resistant to paraphrase and meaningful excerpt than other poetry, all poetry exhibits to a greater or less degree—greatest of all in didactic poetry like the "Essay on Man" and least in "pure" lyrics and the work of certain contemporary symbolists and surrealists—the patterns of assumption, attitude, and idea of the age and of the poet. To discuss the ideas in poetry, then, whether in a close reading of a single poem or in a survey of the recurrent ideas in a body of poems, though it demands more scrupulous regard for context than is required by prose, though

73

it never succeeds in conveying what a poem *is* or even fully what it *means,* is not impossible and may be valuable. Some of the members of the Kenyon school of criticism—the only school we have, and many of us hope that we have learned a little from them—go too far in their zeal to protect poetry from the activities of the barbarian maxim hunters and the obtuse researchers into ideas. If Mr. Eliot's poetry were as devoid of general philosophic significance as some of his followers seem to wish to have it, Mr. Eliot would not be the greatest poet writing in English today, as he obviously is. (One would think that it would have been more generally noticed that one of the several finest things ever written on Mr. Eliot's poetry is Helen Gardner's critical interpretation of the Quartets. The other completely essential piece of criticism that occurs to me at the moment is Cleanth Brooks's interpretation of *The Wasteland.* Which suggests to me that there is room for scaffoldings.)

Without entering further into the vexed question of how to read a poem, I should like to examine the whole body of Mr. Eliot's poetry and prose to try to see to what extent the poet's attitude toward science and scientism has entered into his work. Without for a moment supposing that a prose paraphrase is the equivalent of a poem or that the full meaning of a quotation is evident except to one who has the whole poem in mind, I shall proceed to paraphrase and to quote. It will be found that both Mr. Eliot's poetry and his prose convey a complete condemnation of scientism and on occasion of science, and that his poetry achieves some of its effects by the poet's use of ideas about the world and man drawn from science.

The indictment takes, as I see it, three forms in the

poetry. First, our faith in scientific "facts," our belief that "rational knowledge of causes" will solve our problems, is a mean and pitiable delusion. Second, the abundance of our knowledge has decreased the mystery and banished the splendor of life. And third, scientific philosophies are unbalanced and false, themselves the cause of delusion and wretchedness.

Most often repeated of Mr. Eliot's charges against our scientific age is that of moral blindness. As Robinson charged that we have become Children of the Night because we have put our faith in "factual knowledge of efficient causes" and ceased striving toward the Light, toward self-knowledge and wisdom and awareness of good and evil, so Eliot denounces the age that prizes knowledge above wisdom. "We have suffered far more than a personal loss—We have lost our way in the dark." And as Robinson made his characters turn in vain to scientific books in their search for meaning, as Frost wonders whether psychology has revealed anything essentially new and whether astronomical figures alter the problem of how to achieve the good life, so in Eliot's poetry we find the characters lamenting our blindness: "All our knowledge brings us nearer to our ignorance. . . . Where is the wisdom we have lost in knowledge?"

This deploring of knowledge without wisdom will by some be called obscurantism. But it is obscurantism only if one is convinced, as many are, either that moral choices are really illusory or that neutral scientific knowledge is always used for good ends, the latter belief so patently ridiculous that one can impute it to no one without implying an insult to his intelligence, the former an aspect of that very scientism which is in question. Those who hold to neither of these popular ideas can see point in the poet's lines:

> *The pain of living and the drug of dreams*
> *Curl up the small soul in the window seat*
> *Behind the* Encyclopaedia Britannica.

It is still not fashionable except in very limited circles today to agree with the chorus in *The Rock* when it laments,

> *O weariness of men who turn from God*
> *To the grandeur of your mind . . . to*
> *Dividing the stars into common and preferred,*

but a good many even among those who deplore the poet's piety can agree at least partially with the chorus in *The Family Reunion* when it chants:

> *We understand the ordinary business of living,*
> *We know how to work the machine . . . .*
>
> *But the circle of our understanding is*
> *a very restricted area.*
>
> *Except for a limited number*
> *Of strictly practical purposes*
> *We do not know what we are doing.*

We do not know what we are doing, we are worried, even a little frightened. We turn to science for help and we get—"specifics against insomnia." It is because this is all science has to offer and it is not enough that Mr. Eliot asks us, in *Thoughts After Lambeth,* to "imagine . . . the fatuity of an encyclical letter produced by the joint efforts of Mr. H. G. Wells, Mr. Bernard Shaw, and Mr. Russell; or Professors Whitehead, Eddington, and Jeans;

76

or Dr. Freud, Dr. Jung, and Dr. Adler." It is because fact and value exist in different realms, in his opinion as in Hulme's, that he denies the moral and religious value of those best-selling "peeps into the fairyland of reality," the popular books of Eddington and Jeans. And so, too, he is led to deplore the "excessive amiability" with which the bishops have greeted the scientific books that have religious tendencies. Instead of being deferred to, the religious scientists should be received "as penitents for the sins of an earlier scientific generation." What may be happening "beyond the Heaviside Layer" has little bearing on our problem.

But though the first form of the poet's indictment of an age which has confused fact and value seems to me not to be obscurantism, the second form may be justly so labeled: science has removed the mystery. When "the bright color fades," when the "glow upon the world" departs, it is science that is at fault. One may be reminded of Poe's romantic "Sonnet—To Science" when one reads that in our age the mystery is gone

> *And the eye adjusts itself to a twilight*
> *Where the dead stone is seen to be batrachian,*
> *The aphyllous branch ophidian.*

There can be little doubt that, to a degree at least, the theme in the early poems of the inferiority of the present to the past derives from this nostalgia for the golden day when mystery survived. (Though one must not forget that there is another suggestion, too, in the use of the theme: part of our tragedy is that we are no longer able to *believe* in the "glow," quite apart from the question of whether it actually was present in the past.) When the poet remarks in an essay that we shall all die of boredom after science has reached into every corner, he is expressing an attitude that we have learned to recognize as central in the Romantic movement; it may seem a little odd coming from one who has said so many very unkind things about romanticism.

The third charge is that science has offered us a view of life that is unbelievable and intolerable. It is partly for this reason that we are a "wretched generation of enlightened men" betrayed in the mazes of our own ingenuities. So it is that the modern soul is a "shadow in its own shadows, spectre in its own gloom." The kind of naturalism for which we have given up supernaturalism makes life quite meaningless if it is really believed in. In our eagerness to be modern and realistic, in our determination to believe only in the "publicly observable," we end by denying the significance of value, life, and even the mind that constructed the denial. We end by denying the most significant aspects of our experience. Hence the point of Mr. Eliot's pronouncement that "A purely 'scientific' philosophy ends by denying what we know to be true." Hence also his characterization of behaviorism as an "unbalanced" philosophy. Because our age has typically expressed itself in such "philosophies" as Watsonian behaviorism and popular positivism, we are reduced to shadows in a shadow world of our own construction. Modern secular man, in short, is hollow not simply because he has given up God, but because his own description of himself and of the world leaves no room for any other than hollow men. Mr. Eliot has often implied that he would prefer paganism to our "sub-pagan" scientific culture. For a man of aesthetic and religious sensibilities not to care for a culture which has rendered questions of value and quality meaningless is not, I think, surprising. Even Sidney Hook, philosopher in the positivist and instrumentalist tradition of John Dewey and unfriendly to most of what Mr. Eliot stands for, has warned scientists and philosophers that "popular behaviorism" and "popular psychoanalysis" make questions of value meaningless and that this situation has grave implications.[9]

A part of Mr. Eliot's greatness derives from the fact that he has shown us with wonderful precision what some of the implications of our outlook are. To do so he has made use of modern man's description of himself: this, he has said, is really what you are saying you are, and this, if you *wish* it, *is* what you are.

When Prufrock thinks that he "should have been a pair of ragged claws Scuttling across the floors of silent seas," not only is one's appreciation of Prufrock's irresolution heightened through this ironic contrast with instinctive, prevertebrate "courage," but one's attitude toward Prufrock is influenced in another way: the crustacean is natural, Prufrock human and unnatural. The lucubrations of Mr. Krutch and others on the opposition between the natural and the human are here illustrated in a single line. So also in the description of Bleistein. Another device besides anti-Semitism is here used to make the character repulsive: Bleistein's eyes are not only lustreless and protrusive but they stare "from the protozoic slime." The evolutionary movement is reversed in the description of Bleistein to make him at once repellent and modern.

9 "Storm Signals in American Philosophy," *Virginia Quarterly Review*, Vol. XIV, No. 1 (Winter, 1938), 29–43.

And it is not only in describing the neurotic Prufrocks and the crass Bleisteins that Mr. Eliot makes use
of the picture of a dehumanized man supplied him by
science. In his descriptions of nearly all the lost souls who
inhabit the waste land it is implied that evolutionary development has added nothing new, created nothing; that
human personality is reducible to the mechanisms which
science explores; or that the soul can be discovered, by
scientific analysis, to consist of nothing but blind and
sordid desires or drives or nervous impulses. So in *The
Family Reunion* Harry says:

> *What matters is the filthiness. I can clean my skin,*
> *Purify my life, void my mind,*
> *But always the filthiness, that lies a little deeper.*

And in "Preludes" we may note the same point of view
expressed in lines written some twenty years earlier:

> *You dozed, and watched the night revealing*
> *The thousand sordid images*
> *Of which your soul was constituted.*

Or again, the same general effect is achieved more con-
cisely: "as if a magic lantern threw the nerves in patterns
on a screen." Or in terms of a single word which reduces
the human animal to his prehuman origin: "The silent
vertebrate in brown" withdraws while Rachel "tears at
the grapes with murderous *paws*." Or more diffusely in
a phrase which mimics the jargon of psychoanalysis: "The
natural wakeful life of the Ego is a perceiving." Or as
the chorus in *Murder in the Cathedral* indicates its wise
disillusion with natural life: "I have lain on the floor of
the sea and breathed with the breathing of the sea-ane-
mone, swallowed with the ingurgitation of the sponge."

All these I take to be poetically effective uses of the genetic fallacy.

As Mr. Eliot has used the "nothing but" or "reduction by analysis" mode of modern thought to characterize those people in his poems who live merely on the natural level, so also he has made use of that other horn of the dilemma of modernism, the "alien universe" concept. It may well be that "The effect of popular astronomy books" like those of Sir James Jeans on Mr. Eliot "is only of the insignificance of vast space," but perhaps the sensibility has absorbed what the reasoning mind has rejected, for the alien universe is everywhere in the poems. In "this valley of dying stars" man is dwarfed, lost, rendered ridiculous in his insignificance and feebleness. We are like crickets chirping feebly "through the dust, through the night." When Prufrock wonders whether he dare disturb the universe, the irony is the greater because men of his type are disturbed by thoughts of "De Bailhache, Fresca, Mrs. Cammel, whirled Beyond the circuit of the shuddering Bear In fractured atoms." Despite Mr. Eliot's characterization in his prose of the modern temper of awe in the face of an alien universe as a merely emotional attitude that has found its most sentimental expression in Lord Russell's "A Free Man's Worship," in his poetry he has frequently portrayed men as bits of paper "whirled by the cold wind That blows before and after time." Like many another modern, the poet has felt "the heaving of the earth at nightfall, restless, absurd."

It is this dual sense of the sordidness of man's origins and present nature, as seen from the scientific point of view, and of his homelessness that has helped to convince Mr. Eliot that apart from the revelations of a supernatural faith there is no hope for man. If one considers only the natural facts studied by science, the poet has decided, nihilism is the only possible conclusion. Hence those of his characters who represent the natural man are futile, helpless, hopeless creatures measuring out their lives with coffee spoons, Prufrocks or old men in decayed houses waiting without hope; or they are merely animals, pink bestial Sweeneys. Though modern intellectuals see their heads grow slightly bald, they know that it does not matter, that nothing matters. They know that neither fear nor courage can save them. They have seen fear in a handful of dust and are well aware that their dried voices when they whisper together are quiet and meaningless. They know that they live "in rats' alley Where the dead men lost their bones." And so, in "a world confused and dark and disturbed by portents of fear," with "nothing to do" as they move through "the dream crossed twilight between birth and dying" but "watch the days draw out," they go aimlessly, hopelessly through the motions of living,

> In and out, in an endless drift
> Of shrieking forms in a circular desert
> Weaving with contagion of putrescent embraces
> On dissolving bone.

Mr. Eliot in his poetry has achieved what he has credited to Aldous Huxley's novels: he has shown how sordid a world without a valid philosophy can be.

4. A Poet in a Scientific Age

Certain general observations on the relationship between science and Mr. Eliot's technique are now in order. Certainly no one would argue that the formal nature of Mr. Eliot's poetry could be explained by reference to science. Yet just as surely those detractors of the poet who say or imply that his manner is simply borrowed from the French symbolists are wrong. And when his admirers make him out a "pure" poet, when they ignore or even deny conceptual meaning in his poetry—as though as a man he were living in a vacuum, had severed all connections with his age, and as a poet were careful to keep his verse completely distinct from his life and thought— one begins to wonder what is obvious and what is not.

I think Mr. Brooks is right in saying that the fundamental technique of *The Waste Land* is not irony but its obverse, a collocation of items superficially similar, the basic dissimilarity of which appears only as we become fully acquainted with the items. In Mr. Brooks's words, "The basic method . . . may be described as the application of the principle of complexity."[10] Thus, for example, the Christian meaning of the poem is never stated, but emerges, as Mr. Brooks says, not in spite of but through confusion and cynicism.

The basic justness of this technique should be obvious, but I think has not been sufficiently commented upon. It is not simply a matter of the poet's falling into the "imitative fallacy," expressing confusion by writing confusedly, though I agree with some of the strictures on contemporary experimental poetry made by Mr. Winters.[11] Mr. Eliot is a man of his time. He is fully aware of

[10] Mr. Brooks's analysis is to be found in his *Modern Poetry and the Tradition* (Chapel Hill, 1939); I have used the version reprinted in the B. Rajan collection of essays on Mr. Eliot previously mentioned.

[11] In *Primitivism and Decadence* (New York, 1937).

all the contemporary reasons for disbelief in any supernatural order, both those reasons which we share with
Lucretius and Voltaire and those few that are really new.
He cannot himself achieve a naïve, a straightforward, an
unquestioning belief. He cannot return to the faith of
the Middle Ages, however much he may admire certain
aspects of that period. So it is not simply a matter of strategy—either the positive one of attempting to express confusion by creating confusion, or the negative one of avoiding the clichés of faith that are perhaps not less true now
than they ever were but that we can no longer really hear
—it is not just a question of strategy of art or of persuasion that forces the poet to adopt the indirect, the
complex, the apparently confused way of presenting a
point of view: the complexity of the expression *is* the complexity of the point of view. To achieve a Christian faith
in our time, the manner of the poet's verse is in effect saying, is not only necessary but extremely difficult. Really
to apprehend and hold the faith in our time will require
a struggle in which negation will never be far from affirmation, analytical intelligence from simple assent. Freud
has written and cannot be forgotten: one knows how delusions grow and what wishful thinking is; the anthropologists and the sociologists have shown us the correspondences between our faith and primitive totem and
taboo. Mr. Eliot's charges against science and scientism
are charges that grow from knowledge, not from ignorance, regardless of whether they are justified or not. Anthropology supplied basic structure and much of the material of *The Waste Land* and the impact of psychoanalysis is everywhere discernible in the poems. Full awareness of the import of anthropology and psychoanalysis,

84

not to mention the other sciences, makes a naïve faith impossible.

But there is another aspect of the matter. The parallels between religious rites and symbols studied by anthropology are perfect parallels only to the modernist; to the believer in the moral rightness and realism of Christian theology, the correspondences will seem interesting and expressive but ultimately superficial, masking great differences. As Mr. Toynbee has recently shown us in his great study of history—and his demonstration is impressive to all but those who prefer not to understand him but to dismiss him as dangerously Christian—the similarity of religious myths and symbols and rites often belies their contrasting content. But this contrast of content is apparent only to one who begins by admitting the significance of religious values and the possibility of valid religious insight. To one for whom all religion is superstition, there are, of course, no differences except sociological ones between the many myths of the sacrificial god. So to the casual reader the surface parallels in *The Waste Land* remain parallels and nothing more; and the poem seems confused. And so the poem should have been were there not in it a faith quite sufficient to balance the anthropology, to discern the difference beneath the similarities, to respond to values that do not appear in the questionnaire, the numerical calculation, or the most delicate excavation of ruins.

It is not at all simply a curious accident then that the two books which, more than any others, are at the basis of *The Waste Land* should be *From Ritual to Romance* and *The Golden Bough*. Anthropology includes as one of its subjects the scientific study of the externals of religion.

The structure and content of *The Waste Land* are equivalent to this: Mr. Eliot begins what he has to say about our age by allowing science to suggest the initial structure and the initial content.[12] As new values enter, permutations take place which ultimately twist the symbols to entirely new meanings, in which the anthropological element is submerged in the religious. But science, to repeat, has given the cue. Although he has condemned it, Mr. Eliot has at the same time used science for all it is worth.

But while it is true that the fundamental method of *The Waste Land* is the obverse of irony, it is also true that this and the other poems, the early ones particularly, are marked by irony, and irony of a special sort sometimes called Laforguian. Now irony of this sort has as its special character deflation, diminution. It is in the obvious sense cynical, but its cynicism is of a special kind that depends for its effect upon a dual, or rather an alternating, awareness of fact and value, with value usually having the first and fact the last word. It discovers the horror beneath the fair surface, the role of the genital organs in love, the hidden cancer. Its way of treating facts and values is the parallel in poetry of the genetic or analytical fallacy in scientific philosophy: complex values are explained away by reference to their parts, their mechanisms, their origin. The part, the structure, and the

---

12 Since this chapter was written I have had the pleasure of reading Elizabeth Drew's interesting and valuable book, *T. S. Eliot: The Design of His Poetry* (New York, 1949). Miss Drew finds many interesting parallels between the psychological theories of C. G. Jung and the poetry of T. S. Eliot, and she demonstrates that a reading of the poetry in Jungian terms not only is possible but actually clarifies many otherwise obscure points.

origin are always the "real," the immediately sensed value the illusory. As the Watsonian behaviorist "explained" human behavior by the purely mechanical conditioning of reflexes, so it has become a cliché of much contemporary poetry to juxtapose symbols of value and symbols of fact in such a way that the value symbols are canceled or superseded by the fact symbols. (I shall not enter into the question of what is fact and what is value at this point: I am using the terms in the popular contemporary —to my mind partly mistaken—sense: erotic affection is a value, intercourse a fact; the sense of the beauty, or ugliness, of a poem a value, the number of lines a fact.) The French symbolists were the first to specialize in this sort of irony in modern literature because they responded first to the spirit of our age in a land culturally more advanced along the paths Western culture has been traveling than were England and America. But the positive sense of freedom and freshness with which they were discovered and the faithfulness with which they have been followed long after the novelty has worn off, and by poets who are not mere poetic imitators, suggest that their method is peculiarly appropriate to our age. In a quite literal sense Rimbaud and Laforgue and the rest seemed more contemporary to Ezra Pound and T. S. Eliot, Hart Crane and Archibald MacLeish than living poets like Robinson and Frost or recently dead ones in the English and American tradition. They were contemporary because their method in poetry was an expression of our age of science as Shakespeare's was of Renaissance skepticism and Dante's of medieval Christian faith. Behind the popularity of Laforguian irony in contemporary poetry lies the shaping of our age by science, which has reminded us of our origins, which is interested in efficient, not in final, causes, which treats of facts and is sometimes thought to imply that its treatment is a sufficient coverage of reality. This is the rationale of the Laforguian irony so conspicuous in Mr. Eliot's early poetry.

But the debt to the early symbolists, which is, as I have tried to suggest, at the same time a debt to science, is an aspect of Mr. Eliot's poetry which very easily can be, and I believe sometimes has been, overemphasized. Of the four chief sources of Mr. Eliot's symbols—religious literature, secular literature, contemporary society, and science—science is the least conspicuous; but except for the very early poems, those written before *The Waste Land,* it is more conspicuous than images borrowed from the French. In *The Family Reunion, Murder in the Cathedral,* and *The Rock,* in the Quartets particularly, such symbols as the nerves, the surgeon, astronomical conceptions of space, the rituals studied by anthropology, the earlier forms of life studied by historical geology and biology, details of physiology, dreams and hallucinations of a Freudian cast—all these and others are prominent. They suggest, it is perhaps needless to say, not that the poet has deliberately gone to science for his material, but that he is a part of the age he condemns and that he has grown beyond imitation of his early models even while he has continued in a direction which they first explored.

More significantly, Mr. Eliot's doctrine and practice of the objective correlative is related to the fact that ours is a scientific age. The poet's insistence that his symbols be apprehended in all their fullness and concreteness and that their meaning be intrinsic is an appropriate response to an age when the decay of philosophy and theology has left experimental science in control of the area of discursive reason. Here is no "retreat," properly speaking, as those who are interested in stigmatizing what they consider a "cult of unintelligibility" would have it, but an emphasis on that kind of symbolism most typical of poetry rather than of prose. Yet, though it should not be called a retreat, it seems to me certainly a response, a reaction to a scientific culture. An examination of the chief pieces of theoretical criticism of the years when Mr. Eliot was developing his theory and practice will show that the problem that nearly crowded out all the others was *What can poetry do?* What is its semantic role? Has it any use in an age of science? (It was even asked, seriously, Will it continue in an age of science?) Professor Richards in *The Meaning of Meaning, Science and Poetry,* and other works both symptomatic and influential in the highest degree restricted its function to the organization of our emotions and attitudes, a realm not of meaning but of feeling and action. Many critics and scholars, particularly John Crowe Ransom, Allen Tate, W. M. Urban, T. C. Pollock, Suzanne Langer, and D. G. James[13] have shown what seems to me the utter inadequacy of Mr. Richards' early theories both as poetics and as semantics; but Mr. Richards, a psychologist influenced by both the logical positivists and the behaviorists, was in a position to know

13 John Crowe Ransom, "A Psychologist Looks at Poetry," *The World's Body* (New York, 1938), and "The Psychological Critic," *The New Criticism* (Norfolk, Conn., 1941); Allen Tate, "The Present Function of Criticism," and "Literature as Knowledge," *On the Limits of Poetry* (New York, 1948); W. M. Urban, *Language and Reality* (New York, 1939); T. C. Pollock, "A Theory of Meaning Analyzed," General Semantics Monograph III, Chicago, 1932; Suzanne K. Langer, *Philosophy in a New Key;* and D. G. James, *Scepticism and Poetry* (London, 1937), Chapter 2.

what science was saying about the role of poetry. What he said, and his grounds for saying it, were well known to Mr. Eliot. And Mr. Eliot's early poetry was used by Mr. Richards in his books as a good example of what poetry should be like if it were to exist in an age of science.

There was much in Mr. Eliot's poetry that Mr. Richards missed, but he was right that it was the appropriate poetic response to our age. Surely a moment's reflection will discover interesting parallels between an age of multiplicity, of relativism, and of cultural as well as philosophic atomism and a poetry that insists on facts always, on hard, precise, resistant facts, on truly objective correlatives, that presents simplicity through complexity, that makes the meaning of its symbols a function of the total context. Surely there are striking parallels between a Freudian age and a poetry that utilizes reverie, dream, delirium, and dream symbols, that moves by the relevant irrelevance by which the id expresses itself, a poetry that adopts as its very organizing principle that meaningful confusion which the psychoanalysts have taught us underlies the stratum of our rationality. Perhaps the tremendous influence of Mr. Eliot's attack on our scientific and secular age owes something to the fact that he has borrowed some of his most effective weapons from the enemy.

5. *"The Dry Salvages"*

Although there are many admirers of Mr. Eliot's poetry who feel that his early poems are his best and that *Four Quartets* represents the continuation of a decline that be-

gan in *Ash Wednesday,* when it could no longer be ig-
nored or denied that Mr. Eliot was a religious poet, one
suspects these admirers of responding more readily to
cleverness than to justness—the early poems *are* immensely clever, and more—or of finding any overt expression
of religious conviction or emotion offensive. It seems to
me that the Quartets are Mr. Eliot's finest poetry to date,
that he is, in short, a developing poet. So I should like
to use "The Dry Salvages" to illustrate as many of the
points that I have made in the preceding generalizations
as possible. To analyze the poem from the point of view of
its attitude toward and use of science is, of course, to attempt a highly specialized and incomplete sort of analysis,
a contribution to criticism rather than criticism itself.

I choose this poem fully aware that the obscurity of
the Quartets, though less apparent verbally perhaps, is
really greater than that of the early poems because it reflects the obscurity of the fundamental paradoxes and
mysteries of life rather than that of recondite literary allusion or condensed imagery. I may misinterpret parts
of the poem. But since the Quartets represent the poet's
position at present, and they are, in my opinion, his greatest poems, I shall hazard the difficulties.

Within the structure of the four poems "The Dry Salvages" occupies a climactic position. "Burnt Norton" is
a meditation on time and eternity starting from the "hints
and guesses," the recalled illuminations, afforded by a
garden experience. "East Coker" takes us farther back in
time, beyond the poet's personal experience into ancestral
experience and behind the polished civilization of the
formal garden into a ruder civilization close to the earth's
processes. "The Dry Salvages" takes us beyond civiliza-

91

tion itself into racial experience, and beyond that into the prehuman and the inanimate; it introduces us to the wildness, the vastness, and the terror of the natural universe; it is a "backward look . . . towards the primitive terror." Yet it ends, by a magnificently handled paradox, on a more completely mastered note of Christian humility, resignation, and faith than either of the two preceding poems, and so prepares us for the quiet summing up of the purely religious "Little Gidding." "The Dry Salvages," then, represents the two poles of all the Quartets—the flux and the still point, the terror and the trust —at their point of greatest divergence, yet ends with the completest reconciliation yet achieved. Since I cannot here analyze all four of the poems as, if space permitted, I should like to do, it seems fitting that the choice should be "The Dry Salvages." I should like in what follows to show that the poem makes use of science, judges it, and arrives at a final position on "the place of value in a world of fact."

The opening line, beginning "I do not know much about gods," introduces the poet's usual anthropological note. The river (the Mississippi, the forces of nature close to man, man's life, time) is a "strong brown god," a "reminder of what men choose to forget"—which is, in context, their natural origin and end, their involvement in nature. (Modern man thinks he is dependent, the poem says, neither on nature nor on God.) The poet does not choose to forget the river, although, unlike the naturalists, he does not think it all there is of reality. The "worshippers of the machine," however, do forget the river once it is no longer either a barrier or a problem; paradoxically, the men who worship the machine and in their ruling

philosophy use nature to explain away value, who have
created a picture of the world and of themselves in the
image of the machine with "nature" as their substitute
for religion, nervously occupy themselves with activities
that help them to forget the brown god. But "His rhythm
was present in the nursery bedroom . . . The river is within us." The biological, chemical, and physical forces of
life, the processes alike of stars and tides and digestion,
are within us; our involvement in nature is such that no
denial of the brown god can alter the fact of his presence.
(The prose level of meaning here has been proved physio-
logically by Lawrence J. Henderson's *Fitness of the Environment,* which shows that it is difficult to tell where
organism ends and environment begins.)

But the river merges into the second chief symbol of
the poem, the sea. River and sea are at once the same and
different: nature as temporal, in flux, and nature as eternal, or, more strictly, relatively permanent; nature as human and as subhuman, nature in its closer and in its more
remote aspects. The symbolism here is too complex to
explicate in less than a full essay devoted to this part
of the poem alone, but it should be noted at least that
river and sea merge, that despite their real differences
they are ultimately equivalent in the poem. And so what
is washed up on the beach at the sea's edge—the "hints
of earlier and other creation," the starfish, the hermit
crab, the algae and the sea anemone—is what is potential
in the river, is the sea's equivalent of the "dead Negroes,
cows, and chicken coops" on the surface of the river
which, in flood, has reasserted its presence. Man is a part
of nature, as the naturalists say, though not precisely in
the way they mean it; he is cousin to the sea anemone,

the river is within us, and the most ingenious gadgets, the most incessant distractions, do nothing to alter the fact. "The salt is on the briar rose"; love, our highest value, grows out of natural conditions even while it gives us a glimpse of the supernatural—for the sea whose salt is on the rose is an ambiguous symbol which points at once to time and to eternity, to the most frightening and alien aspects of nature and to the permanence in the midst of change which is one of God's attributes. (The salt on the brier rose, though it "means" in part that love is the product of physiology, is not a specimen of Laforguian irony. No self-depreciation, no substitution of fact for value, no cynical diminishment is conveyed by this complex symbol which suggests at once love's natural and —ultimately, though not at this point in the poem—its supernatural being.)

To retrace our steps for a moment, the "hints of earlier and other creation" should be compared with the "superficial notions of evolution" which in the second part of Section II are said to encourage the "partial fallacy" of seeing history as development, as progress. There has been development in some areas, along some lines, the poem says, but not a straightline "progress," belief in which is our way of disowning the past. History—to skip ahead to Section II—is in the profoundest sense neither cyclical nor straight-line evolutionary, but a chaotic darkness of change and decay, a flux and a forgetting in which what is forgotten still lives, a darkness illumined here and there by experiences which we missed the meaning of at the moment, epiphanies recalled but seldom perceived. (This interpretation of history suggests Arnold Toynbee's and is to that extent revolutionary, not, as

94

some have come to expect all of Mr. Eliot's ideas to be, either traditional or conservative.)

The sea whose salt is on the briar rose has many voices, the sea howl and the sea yelp, the sounds of the groaner and the gull, the whine in the rigging; but all of these are contrasted with and give way in the order of the poem to the tolling bell which "Measures time not our time, rung by the unhurried Ground swell." All these voices are real, needless to say, but the bell, with its many values, values which change as the poem proceeds—it later merges with the bell that calls to worship and so suggests faith, though it here suggests death—the bell is rung by a ground swell, swings to a profounder rhythm than those of storm and calm. It is the first distinctly religious symbol in the poem, though its religious values become really apparent only later. In the perspective of the whole poem, I should say, trying to summarize fluid symbolic values that do not lend themselves to prose summary without distortion, the bell suggests that there is an approach to God through nature, as there is also an approach which sheds, destroys, or forgets nature; a positive as well as a negative approach. "The way up is the way down." (The bell symbolism shows, I think, as does the sympathetic passage which follows on the "anxious worried women," a development of the poet toward attitudes not popularly associated with him. There is no "negativism" here.) Yet one must quickly note that the bell offers only an approach to God, a reminder of His presence. It is indeed even an approach only insofar as it takes us out of ourselves, enlarges our perspective, and hints that there is other reality than the Heraclitian flux.

The beautiful lyric which opens Section II of the

poem begins with the question, "Where is there an end of it?" and concludes with the answer, the Annunciation—an answer hinted at with ever increasing clarity throughout a series of plays on the word and the idea of annunciation but withheld in statement until the last word of the lyric. This is the turning point of the poem: out of fact, the facts of river and sea, the facts of dead Negroes and primitive life, out of the many voices and the many rhythms of nature, value has emerged. "The backward look," then, of the second part of Section II has already proved its value by the time it is discussed in the prosy lines beginning, "It seems, as one becomes older." The two sides of nature have been suggested—"Time the destroyer is time the preserver," "the bitter apple and the bite in the apple"—and their contradictions have been reconciled in the Annunciation. The "ragged rock in the restless waters"—and how many symbolic values this rock has—is always there, is "what it always was." Here, then, is a reinforcement and development of the symbol of the bell tolled by the ground swell: permanence in change, a source of terror but also of comfort, a hard, resistant, unyielding, cruel—"Christ the tiger"—but also infinitely precious fact. Here, in this rock, fact and value merge as we now see they did in the briar rose, but with more decisive results: the rock does not, like the rose, suggest transience.

I share Miss Gardner's feeling that the third section is somewhat weakened by its dependence on Indian scriptures, since the ideas which are attributed to Krishna may be found within the Christian tradition unmixed with the element of negative detachment or quietism. But for our present purposes the section has a special significance:

again, as in *The Waste Land,* we see the poet searching
for unhackneyed expressions of Christian doctrine; we
see him expressing a point of view indirectly partly because a direct expression of it would not be attended to
and partly because the point of view itself is the result
of an intellectual search.

The Lyric which makes up Section IV is a simple yet
rich and moving prayer, an expression of the humility,
resignation, and faith at which the poem has arrived
through meditation and lyric. Once more I should like
to suggest that we see here a very different spirit from that
which is so prominent in Mr. Eliot's early poems, like
the clever but certainly not great "Morning at the Window," with its condescension toward the "damp souls of
housemaids." The struggle to apprehend the faith has
not been entirely fruitless: out of it has grown greater
charity. "Morning at the Window" is a naturalistic poem,
the prayer here is Christian; there is a practical, a theoretical, and a formal difference.

The final, prosaic, meditative section of the poem
begins with the dismissal of science as merely one of the
many distractions by which modern man keeps his mind
off the central questions and his emotions safe from the
saving terror. The question of obscurantism again arises,
as I have suggested it always does in relation to Mr. Eliot's
attitude toward science; but it is noteworthy that it is
not all of science, nor science seen from all points of view,
that is dismissed. "To communicate with Mars," to "fid-
dle with pentagrams Or barbituric acids, or dissect The
recurrent image into preconscious terrors," these are the
equivalent of an earlier age's magic and divination, these
are the signs of our anxiety and our need for distraction.

The barbiturates are sedative drugs; they do not cure but merely hide the malady. So, too, in the glance at psychoanalysis the dismissal is aimed not at the science as a whole but at those uses of it which conceal or deny the moral and religious problem whose solution must await recognition that the problem exists. (Like Dr. Jung, Mr. Eliot would apparently suggest here that there is a revelation in the "recurrent image" which is not to be gainsaid by Freudian genetic analysis.) There is, in short, no condemnation here of science as such, but only of those activities and interests, scientific and unscientific, which prevent man from attending to the bell, from seeking the still point. If, as the poem says a little later, attending to the vision is "an occupation for the saint," and so an occupation which most of us, not being saints, can hardly hope to pursue successfully, yet we can respect it when it does occur; and we shall not respect it if we follow the cue of popular interpretations of science, if we rely on the barbiturates and spend our curiosity on Mars. We shall not respect it, nor shall we attend even to those "hints and guesses" which are for most of us the only personal revelation, nor shall we be led to "the rest": to "prayer, observance, discipline, thought, and action." Science, then, is dismissed only insofar as it distracts us from reality or denies or discredits that reality: this is obscurantism only in the view of the naïve positivists whose attitudes reflect the scientism of the twenties but who still frequently pass as enlightened in our day.

The closing lines of the poem, with their acceptance of the "temporal reversion," take us back to the opening, to the river and the sea. The ending is quiet, humble, and deeply Christian.

> *We, content at the last*
> *If our temporal reversion nourish*
> *(Not too far from the yew-tree)*
> *The life of significant soil.*

Thus the poem ends as it begins, on the theme of nature: the river, the soil. But this soil is not pagan earth; here is a symbol at once parallel to and quite distinct from the brown god. The dynamic stresses of the poem have worked their alterations in the symbols so that we now see nature in a different light. The nature which opens the poem is the nature of pagan naturalism; this is a soil enriched not by soil chemistry but by a grasp of values which include and transcend naturalism. This is *significant* soil. The significance has been found in the realm of value, of which science says nothing or the wrong things. The poem which begins with that part of the pagan vision which is permanently true ends with the Christian vision, which does not so much deny as complete paganism. The poem which begins in anthropology ends in Christian faith and hope. The anthropology, I repeat, has not been denied; rather, its significance has been found within a system of values. (The basic structure here is like that of *The Waste Land*.) Science and paganism are finally affirmed, not dismissed. Those who have talked about the poet's turning his back on all modern knowledge in what they take to be a frightened retreat had better read his verse again.

6. *Naturalism and Supernaturalism*

In "Second Thoughts about Humanism," Mr. Eliot's chief criticism of the sort of humanism of which he took

Norman Foerster as representative was that humanism of this variety, failing to take account of the special authority of the supernatural, tries at once to derive comfort from religion (without believing in religious dogmas) and authority from science (without being willing to go the whole way with the scientists and erect a thoroughly naturalistic ethics).

I can understand, though I do not approve, the naturalistic systems of morals founded upon biology and analytical psychology (what is valid in these consists largely of things that were always known); but I cannot understand a system of morals which seems to be founded on nothing but itself— which exists, I suspect, only by illicit relations with either psychology or religion or both, according to the bias of mind of the individual humanist.

The choice before modern man, then, is between naturalism and supernaturalism. Humanism that is not merely a subordinate aspect of revealed religion will not do:

Man is man because he can recognize supernatural realities, not because he can invent them. Either everything in man can be traced as a development from below, or something must come from above. There is no avoiding that dilemma: you must be either a naturalist or a supernaturalist.

Sidney Hook, in his warning to scientists that for their own good and the good of society they should not forget that the most important questions in life are questions not of number but of value, made the point a few years ago that

The empiricists must . . . work out a scientific approach to values which will not end in the strange conclusion that value judgments are meaningless, and so drive those for whom ethical values and principles *are* meaningful into the arms of authoritarianism to save their moral sanity.

To many Mr. Eliot will seem the perfect example of those morally sensitive people who have been driven into "authoritarianism" to save their moral sanity. But as I said of Mr. Frost, a sympathetic commentary would interpret Mr. Eliot's progress not as a flight but as a seeking. As he himself has said,

> *In a world of fugitives*
> *The person taking the opposite direction*
> *Will appear to run away.*

But it is very easy to overemphasize the reactionary aspects of his development. Though he has in some respects sharpened the dichotomy between natural law and human will, between matter and mind, fact and value, the natural and the supernatural, yet the type of supernaturalism which he has espoused is very far indeed from being "pure faith," whatever that would be. His Christianity is in the great tradition; it has room within it for all the manifestations of man's curiosity and his effort to control his environment, it has room for science. It is not Puritanism, moralism, or frontier evangelicalism. The *facts* which the natural sciences have discovered can be accommodated within the system of belief which contradicts some of the conclusions too hastily drawn by the wishful thinking of materialistic generations—such as the conclusion of the Watsonians that man has neither mind nor soul, memory nor will. Though Mr. Eliot has yet to speak a kind word for Emerson, and though he has gone in the opposite direction from Emerson's effort to redeem the natural by seeing it as the manifestation of the divine, yet his search "at the still point of the turning world . . . Where past and future are gathered" for the consciousness which is not in time was Emerson's search, as it was Bergson's. With Robinson, he has sought the light which would illumine the darkness of our life; and although the light which he has found is very different from any that Robinson could conceive as being valid for our time, the two agree that

> *Time past and time future*
> *Allow but a little consciousness.*
> *To be conscious is not to be in time.*

Again he has asked, with Emerson, Robinson, and Bergson, in Bergsonian language, "*When* will time flow away?" And his answer has echoed the answers of those very idealists in the chief American philosophic tradition with whom the poet has in most respects so decisively broken:

> *Time past and time future*
> *Point to one end, which is always present.*

It is, then, finally with the popular positivists, the popular behavioristic semanticists, and other spokesmen for materialism, whether dialectical or not, that Mr. Eliot has an absolute quarrel; for these groups would deny the very point of any distinction between time and eternity, the physical and the spiritual, fact and value. The whole body of Mr. Eliot's work, both the poetry and the criticism, has grown from the reaction of an aesthetic and religious sensibility to our scientific secular age. If those who hold that value judgments are subjective or meaningless are right, then there is no valid conceptual basis for any of the poet's work, or for that of any poet or prophet. If they are right, then the poet's life work looks something like a compulsive flight from reality, the defense mechanism of a neurotic personality. This may be what it is. I think the issue should be clearly drawn, the alternatives recognized. Value judgments in art and religion and other aspects of life are either real and in some sense public, or they are merely data to be studied by psychoanalysis, neurotic or psychotic symptoms. If they have some validity other than merely statistical, they may still be subjects for analytical study; but the materialists and the positivists will not be right about them: they will not be "merely" something else.

This is the issue, whether one agrees with Mr. Eliot in his naturalist-supernaturalist alternative or not. One's position on this question will certainly influence his judgment of Mr. Eliot's worth as a poet, no matter how loudly one insists that art and propaganda are not one.

But in the end I think most of us will agree on one thing, however great our philosophic differences: Mr. Eliot's poetry was thirty years ago and is today right for our time. For it has grown from the facts of a scientific age as a tree grows from rocky soil, searching out the crevices between the rocks, seeking significant soil under and beyond the rocks, adapting itself to an environment that will support growth but does not nourish passivity. The strength of the poet's reaction is in direct proportion to the nature of an environment created for other ends than the production of poetry and the nourishment of religion. These are the roots that have clutched, these the branches that have grown out of this stony rubbish.

Mr. Eliot's poetry is contemporary, it is traditional, and it is reactionary. To understand it fully, one must understand what it has reacted from as well as what it has sought to find in the trilling wire in the blood, within the garlic and the sapphires, behind the dance along the artery and the circulation of the lymph, at the still point.

V. Robinson Jeffers:
Here is Reality

> *Poetry . . . always says certain things . . . about*
> *man and about human life. . . . [Its assertions]*
> *are about persons. This may seem the veriest plati-*
> *tude, but it is, properly understood, of the utmost*
> *significance. For science . . . never speaks of per-*
> *sons and has no interest in them as such.*
> —W. M. URBAN *in* Language and Reality

1. *A Poetry Powerful and Real*

When some ten years ago Mr. Jeffers came to write a foreword to a volume of his selected poems, he refrained from taking issue with his critical enemies and limited himself to explaining the origin of the poems in the volume. Dismissing his first two books as preparatory exercises, he told how he had gradually arrived at his mature position through his discovery of Nietzsche's dictum that "The poets lie too much" and through his distaste for the products of the French symbolists and their contemporary followers. We can see what Mr. Jeffers meant by the "lies" in the older poetry when we look into his own first two volumes. And we can see what he meant— though most of us are not likely to agree—when he called the poetry of the symbolist tradition "slight and fantastic, abstract, unreal, eccentric." But how he was to write poetry which would not "lie" or be slight, fantastic, and so on is a more interesting question. What did Mr. Jeffers

105

consider the alternative to Victorian poetic "idealism" and to the newly discovered symbolism of Mr. Eliot?

The Foreword itself supplies what is meant as an answer, though the meaning of the words becomes clear only after we have read the verse. Long before any of the poems included in the volume of selections was written, says Mr. Jeffers, it became evident to him that "poetry —if it was to survive at all—must reclaim some of the power and reality it was so hastily surrendering to prose." (Here we have again the question that bemused Mr. Richards: Can poetry survive in an age of science?)

Power and *reality,* yes, certainly—but how was one to achieve power, and what is reality? Without directly answering these questions, Mr. Jeffers went on to say that the feeling that verse must have power and reality led him to write narrative poetry, to draw subjects from contemporary life, to present aspects of life that modern poetry had generally avoided, and "to attempt the expression of philosophic and scientific ideas in verse." Would not these subjects, Mr. Jeffers implied, make his verse powerful and its content real?

But powerful verse is not made simply by powerful subjects, and the nature of the real is not finally clarified by saying *contemporary, philosophic,* and *scientific.* How Mr. Jeffers has attempted to achieve power in his verse, in addition to choosing powerful subjects, will appear in due time, but what the essence of the real is in his poetry may be stated immediately:

> *Before the first man*
> *Here were the stones, the ocean, the cypresses,*
> *And the pallid region in the stone-rough dome*
> *of fog where the moon*

Falls on the west. Here is reality.
The other is a spectral episode: after the
inquisitive animal's
Amusements are quiet: the dark glory.

The real, then, is to be found in the dark glory, not in
the spectral episode. Here is the key to Mr. Jeffers' verse,
to its "meaning" and ultimately to its "form," to many
of its faults and perhaps to some of its virtues. For as a
man judges what is real, so will he think—and write.
(Though conviction and temperament, reason and cir-
cumstance, may be out of harmony, of course. Man does
not think or write by conviction alone.) The unreasoned
nominalism of our age obscures the fact, but ideas do have
consequences.[1]

2. *Aspects of Reality*

What can it mean to say that reality lies in the dark glory
of the inanimate or the preconscious and that man is a
spectral episode? How can "nature," which is a part of
man's experience, be more real than man's whole experience? If man and his mind are but a momentary disease
of matter, how can one trust one's judgment about what
is real? These seem knotty problems.

But it is not, after all, nature as experienced by man
that is finally real, but nature as studied by the natural
sciences. The universe of scientific discourse is not simply
another realm of discourse: it is the reality behind the

[1] Not always in the way or to the extent that Richard Weaver has
recently tried to demonstrate in *Ideas Have Consequences* (Chicago,
1948), which seems to me extreme and inaccurate in some of its analyses.
My own position is comparable to that of Whitehead in *Adventures of
Ideas* (New York, 1933).

appearance. We need not rely on perception: science has shown us the truth, and the truth it has shown us, partly perceptible, partly not, is Reality.

This real universe, so the views expressed in Mr. Jeffers' poetry go, is alien to man, not alien in the sense that man has originated from extra-natural sources, but alien to that part of his humanity which he prizes most, alien to the contagion of consciousness and the delusion of values. The size of the universe, the vastness of its time scale, and the "inhumanness" of its processes as described by the physical sciences make it alien or "indifferent."[2] It is alien—and so terrifying—in precisely the manner and for the reasons described by the late Sir James Jeans in his summary of the old and the new outlooks in science. Of the imaginative and emotional effects of what he considered the old and invalid outlook he had this to say:

> Standing on our microscopic fragment of a grain of sand, we attempt to discover the nature and purpose of the universe which surrounds our home in space and time. Our first impression is something akin to terror. We find the universe terrifying because of its inconceivably long vistas of time which dwarf human history to the twinkling of an eye, terrifying because of our extreme loneliness, and because of the material insignificance of our home in space—a millionth part of a grain of sand out of all the sea-sand in the world.

2 Mr. Jeffers in a letter to the writer some years ago preferred the word "indifferent," since, he said, man is a *natural* product of the earth's chemistry, even though a brief and insignificant one. Just how the wholly improbable "spectral episode" came into being in a world of probability, a world in which all phenomena but those of life seem to obey the second law of thermodynamics, Mr. Jeffers did not think it necessary to try to explain. His letter is quoted in my "Science and the Poetry of Robinson Jeffers," *American Literature,* Vol. X, No. 3 (November, 1938), 257–88.

But above all else, we find the universe terrifying because it appears to be indifferent to life like our own; emotion, ambition, and achievement, art and religion all seem equally foreign to its plan. . . . Into such a universe we have stumbled, if not exactly by mistake, at least as the result of what may properly be described as an accident.[3]

Sir James dismissed this view of things as no longer warranted by the facts, but Mr. Jeffers will have nothing to do with what he considers the recent wishful reinterpretation of science. "What is humanity in this cosmos?" he asks in *Roan Stallion*. And he has the answer always ready: "a moment's accident," a "heresy" of the slime, "the last least taint of a trace in the drugs of the solution." The "speckled Tissues" of the universes are wild and beautiful; they will not note man's passing. From the first man to the last, from the first life even to the final dark and cold that will come with the cooling of the sun, will be but an instant of real time. Measured in light years, the history of life on the planet is truly seen: it hardly exists at all. And as for mankind: "Seen from this height they are shrunk to insect size." Outside the human mind, in the dark beautiful reality, there is no thought, no meaning, only facts: "a certain measure in phenomena: The fountains of the boiling stars, the flowers on the foreland, the ever-returning roses of dawn."

In this reality of physical fact, life has somehow appeared, and man, the inquisitive animal. And as the reality of the universe is discovered by consulting astronomy, physics, and chemistry, so whatever reality man may lay claim to is found by consulting biophysics and biochemistry, neurology, behavioristic psychology, and

[3] *The Mysterious Universe* (New York, 1933), 3–4.

psychoanalysis. It is found, that is, in a study of those functions, mechanisms, and processes which man shares with the gaseous nebulae and the falling of weights—or, at any rate (one skips lightly over the difference here) with the flowers on the foreland and the hawks above the cliffs. Man is really nothing but "the beast that walks upright, with speaking lips And little hair," the "inquisitive animal," the "filthiest of beasts," the absurd "animalcule." But to call man an animal and nothing more is simply to be a naturalist; the reduction here goes further. "The animals Christ was rumored to have died for" are (unlike real animals) simply their physics and chemistry:

> One people, the stars and the people, one structure;
>   the voids between the stars, the voids between
>   the atoms, and the vacancy
> In the atom in the rings of the spinning demons,
> Are all full of that weaving.

The chemistry of the stars and the chemistry of the cells is the same chemistry. Man, as Mr. Jeffers says elsewhere, is the scum on the edge of the warm sea, the contagion in the sane and beautiful inanimate, the moment's aberration. His traditional moral standards are instinctive, irrational, or clever habits and customs; aesthetic values are as unimportant in the sum total of things as ethical values ("divinely superfluous beauty" is everywhere in nature, but it is small comfort or help to the little animal); and religion is sheer delusion. God, freedom, and immortality, said Kant; the superfluous beauty, the chemical necessity, and obliteration, says Mr. Jeffers. Man is nothing but . . . what, shall we say? "We need nothing," wrote John B. Watson, founder and leader of the behaviorists when

Mr. Jeffers was writing some of the poems that brought him to the height of his reputation, "We need nothing to explain behavior but the ordinary laws of physics and chemistry."[4]

To recognize this reality for what it is—and it is such a simple reality that one wonders why it was not recognized long ago—to see it plainly and still to keep one's peace of mind requires that one renounce his humanity. (As many reviewers have remarked, there are interesting parallels between Mr. Jeffers' outlook and certain aspects of the higher religions.) One must give one's heart to the hawks. One might suppose it not difficult to give up the bad dream, the instant of pain; but the incestuous little beast is in love with himself and actually appears to cherish the nightmare. He must learn, painfully and slowly, first to value the hawks and the stallions above men, then to value stones above stallions and hawks. I have said *above,* but the ladder of values leads downward, not up; the simpler, the more real; the more real, the more valuable. Hawks are better than men because they are more natural; stones are more natural still. The beauty of hawks, the peace of stones, these must come to be the objects of our contemplation (but not of our desire, for to desire is to strive, and to strive is human and useless).

Religion has, of course, often used terms almost like these; it has even counseled similar action: control or obliterate the desires, die to the self, love the God who transcends all human imaginings. But the Christian religion, unlike the Indian, has turned all this counsel of death to the purposes of a fuller life; it has denied the humanistic only to achieve what it has conceived to be

4 *The Battle of Behaviorism* (London, 1928), 27.

the more fully human. This, according to Mr. Jeffers' verse, is its delusion. This is what makes it not merely false but harmful. Mr. Jeffers has given his account of the nature of the savior complex and of the mechanism of belief in saviors. The account is Freudian in substance and in result; it relieves us of the necessity of taking religion seriously. ("In our view the truth of religion may be altogether disregarded," wrote Freud toward the end of his career.[5]) But Mr. Jeffers does not invariably disregard in his verse the question of the truth or falsity of religion. He has serious philosophical objections to Christianity and now and then he has expressed them in his poems, as in the passage in "Apology for Bad Dreams" which begins:

> He brays humanity in a mortar to bring the savor
> From the bruised root: a man having bad dreams,
>   who invents victims, is only the ape of that God.
> He washes it out with tears and many waters, calcines
>   it with fire in the red crucible,
> Deforms it, makes it horrible to itself: the spirit
>   flies out and stands naked, he sees the spirit,
> He takes it in the naked ecstasy; it breaks in his
>   hand, the atom is broken, the power that
>   massed it
> Cries to the power that moves the stars, "I have come
>   to myself, behold me."

(This seems to me bad prose as well as bad verse.) But there is usually no more argument in this poetry than there is on the other side of the question in Mr. Eliot's. Each simply assumes a reality which seems to him self-

5 New Introductory Lectures on Psychoanalysis (New York, 1933), 229.

evident. Besides, one does not argue with those who seem stupid or ignorant ("My father," wrote Mr. Jeffers some years ago, "was a clergyman but also intelligent."[6]), though one may on occasion briefly state one's reasons for differing with the many, as in the passage which follows the summary of Christ's significance in "Apology for Bad Dreams":

> *I have seen these ways of God: I know of no reason*
> *For fire and change and torture and the old returnings.*
> *He being sufficient might be still. I think they admit*
>   *of no reason; they are the ways of my love.*
> *Unmeasured power, incredible passion, enormous*
>   *craft: no thought apparent but burns darkly*
> *Smothered with its own smoke in the human*
>   *brain-vault: no thought outside: a certain*
>   *measure in phenomena. . . .*

The remarkable phrase in these lines seems to me to be "they are the ways of my love." I am reminded of the struggle which Jonathan Edwards had to go through before he could accept the ways of a sovereign God: with his deity defined by science rather than by the Bible and Christian tradition, Mr. Jeffers suggests that one may come through a difficult discipline to love the void, to cherish the thing that denies one's humanity. Here, too, is a reminder that Mr. Frost's strategy is not peculiar to him, that it is, in fact, a permanent aspect of human experience, a part of the painful process of maturing. Here also is a kind of inversion of the progress of the saints that Mr. Eliot has described so beautifully. It is this essentially religious emotion informing so much of Mr. Jeffers' verse

---

[6] In a letter to the writer. Quoted by permission in the article on Mr. Jeffers mentioned in n. 2 above.

that seems to me often to be the chief source of the power and dignity of verse that otherwise frequently suggests a feebly rhetorical hymn to chemistry.

But what all this means, finally, is that Mr. Jeffers is the victim of what Whitehead has called the fallacy of misplaced concreteness. The abstract knowledge obtained in the physics or the chemistry laboratory he finds concrete, descriptive of the real; the concrete data of experience, the feeling, the flow, the quality, he concludes—and quite rightly if his first conclusion is correct—must be somehow illusory. This, as F. H. Bradley remarked long ago, is barbarous metaphysics.

3. Form as Experience

In 1912, Mr. Jeffers published a little volume of lyrics concerned mostly with "the infinite pain of love and the joy of the pain." Most poets when young have written verse which they later regretted, and to call the youthful efforts to public attention may be an act of unkindness. But there are critical situations in which it is necessary to recall a poet's early verse, not to discredit his later achievement but to proceed with a serious analysis of his mature work. One of the lyrics in *Flagons and Apples* is called "To Aileen-of-the-Woods," and its title, which is not ironical, and its first two lines enable one to guess what will follow. It begins:

> *Loveliest, there lie inside your eyes*
> *Marvels of ever new surprise.*

And a little later it attributes to the eyes the power of calling up memories of the "clean, wild passions of the woods"; the eyes, it appears, "are springs of those old dreams You gave me once by woodland streams."

Now apart from the fact that the lyric is a tissue of clichés—one expects them in the borrowed language of a poetic exercise, though not perhaps so concentrated as here—apart also from the fact that this poetry springs from the late-nineteenth-century tradition worked by Bliss Carman and others, there is something about the poem, as about the others in the volume, which to one acquainted with Mr. Jeffers' mature verse will seem remarkable: the eyes, physical objects, are treated as having intangible values. It does not particularly matter that the values are trite and perhaps half false, not so much experienced as lifted from other poems. (These are perhaps among the "lies" that Mr. Jeffers learned from Nietzsche to avoid.) What matters is that there are objects here seen in terms of human values.

When Mr. Jeffers had found his mature manner, after his second volume, and had learned not to "lie" in poetry, he gave up not simply the false values, or the false emphases in the values, but values altogether. His discovery that the poets lie was equivalent to a discovery that poets work with human values. So when he treats "love" in his mature poetry, he treats it like this:

> . . . *for she had to believe this passion*
> *Not the wild heat of nature, but the superstitiously*
>   *worshipped spirit of love*
> . . . *she adorned the deed with the dream it needed*
> . . . *her nerve cells intermitted their human dream;*
> *The happy automatism of life, inhuman as the*
>   *sucking of the whirlpool, usurped the whole*
>   *person,*
> *Aping pain, crying out and writhing like torture.*

The change here is deeper than that from traditional to free verse, deeper than that from a literary to a scientific vocabulary: it is a change of attitude from one that accepts value as real to one that explains it away (a dream) by analyzing the facts and mechanisms that accompany or produce it. The passage from *Thursoe's Landing* suggests that love is nothing but a dream that "adorns" the reality, which is pure mechanism. After his first two volumes Mr. Jeffers learned, as he said, to deal with the *real* in his poems.

His discovery of the real may be traced in the language of his verse as well as in the total intention of the poems.[7] In the early poems the significant words are symbols of experienced objects and states: eyes, woods, coast, sea, love, beauty, summer, stars; and their modifiers: lovely, harsh, beautiful, lonely. In the later volumes the objects and states remain, but are radically transformed by a context determined by words of a different type. No one has ever experienced an electron, though it is possible to see the trace it presumably has left on a photographic plate; no one has ever experienced the glowing of a ganglion. (The picture of the brain as essentially a very complicated telephone exchange without operators is a reflection of the spirit of our age rather than an interpretation of experimental evidence.) In short, in the later poetry there has been added a large group of symbols of a different type, symbols not of experienced reality but of scientific "constructs." When Mr. Jeffers sprinkles his verse

[7] In the article on Mr. Jeffers referred to above, I have summarized the ways in which the influence of the several sciences has affected Mr. Jeffers' poetic vocabulary. For a general discussion of science in the poetry, see L. C. Powell, *Robinson Jeffers, The Man and His Work* (Los Angeles, 1934).

with *autolytic enzymes, ganglia, somatic cells, coronal suture, protons, systole, nerve-pulp,* and the like, he is declaring his belief about the locus of reality; and the addition of these symbols is sufficient to transform the others. *Beauty* becomes *superfluous beauty* (beauty is superfluous in the laboratory), *love* a *dream* produced as a kind of afterthought by the automatism of the tissues. If, seen from a great height, man is shrunk to insect size, so experience looked at in a context provided by chemistry or physics is shrunk to laboratory size. The scientific terms and allusions in Mr. Jeffers' mature poetry provide the essential element of the context in which the objects, events, states, and all the rest must be interpreted. The real has been found, and the discovery is momentous: it alters everything.

In neither the early nor the late poetry is the technique that of the objective correlative. Mr. Jeffers' poetry has always tended to be discursive. The early volumes, though romantic in several senses, are filled with words denoting experiences, the later with words denoting scientific theories; in neither is there that symbolic immediacy which we have learned to expect in contemporary poetry. And this "technical" fact is related to the philosophic fact. For after he had learned not to imitate the worn conventions of late Victorian poetry, Mr. Jeffers found reality in science, and in a particular set of scientific attitudes and assumptions which, as Whitehead has shown for once and for all, implied a denial of the competing realities of life, mind, and value. In discursive symbols borrowed from the scientific disciplines, then, and with an outlook which grants at best a grudging and temporary reality to the concrete data of consciousness, Mr. Jeffers has attempted to avoid the "lies" of poetry.

The result has been that his famous long narratives, though violent and sensational in their material, are highly diffuse as poetry. They go round and round their object, whether that object be a condemned man's experiences, the torture of a horse, incestuous sexual intercourse, or simply a sunset. They go round and round, unable to *present,* repetitiously analyzing the mechanism while the event itself never quite becomes real. For these are stories in verse dealing with people; only as the people are human can they engage our sympathy and hold our interest. The inadequately human creatures in Mr. Jeffers' narrative poems have had their "personalities" evaporated away until only the mechanisms of personality are left. We are told of the wish-fulfilling delusions, the movements of the electrons in their brains, the production of adrenalin in moments of excitement. But in fiction and poetry adrenalin is not more but less real than anger and fright. What we experience is anger, not adrenalin; it is not even clear that adrenalin *causes* anger (that is the very point at issue between the scientific mechanists and the antimechanists). To describe anger in terms of adrenalin, then, is equivalent in poetry to describing a book in terms of the processes of the manufacture of paper or a recording of a Mozart piece in terms of the physics of sound. It is not only in no sense true that sound waves are more "real" than music, but it is even arguable that sound waves are so limited an abstraction from the complex whole that is music that a discussion of them is quite irrelevant to music. So, too, if a novelist or a poet is to make his characters real to us, is indeed even to make them characters at all in the proper sense, he must show us their anger and their fright. So also with love, which as the sexual act, as desire, and as "overestimation of the sexual object"[8] occupies so prominent a place in Mr. Jeffers' poems. It may be useful to the psychologist to define the emotional and intellectual experience commonly called love as overestimation of the sexual object, but that is not what love is to the person experiencing it. It is not even what it is to an outsider; it is what it is for the purposes of certain contemporary psychologies. And there is a sense in which the reader of a narrative poem must feel a connection between his own experiences and that of the characters; which is not to say that he must identify himself wholly with the characters. We know nothing about the ganglions of Ulysses or Hamlet; we know a good deal about them as human beings, we recognize our common humanity in them. Precisely because Mr. Jeffers has misplaced the real—in an artistic sense certainly, and in a philosophic sense, too, in my judgment —the characters in his poems are for the most part not real.

The fact that he has taken both the general outlines of his view of human nature and the specific terms of his analysis of it from psychologies commonly held to be valid does nothing to improve the quality of his narratives as poetry. Man lives by valuation; he has an illusion —if such it be—of identity, of *self*-ness, of personality, of being a changing yet enduring and dynamic force as well as the product and recipient of forces; he has even thought in earlier ages that he had a soul. But the chief effort of modern psychology, and not only of Watsonian behavior-

8 The term is Freud's.

ism, has been to imitate biology and physics by giving a genetic and mechanical explanation of these experienced or assumed realities, to dissolve them into the scientific "facts" which are assumed to give rise to the illusion of their existence. Love, says psychology, is just a "positive response" to an object or a person, that is, when it is not "overestimation." Morals are nothing but customs or mores, completely relative, matters of taste and accident.[9] These definitions suggest exactly the forms which love and morality take in Mr. Jeffers' mature poems. But definitions which cover equally well, and without any modification, love and hate (both are "positive responses"), alms-giving and the execution in gas chambers in concentration camps of people innocent of any wrong (both have been "customs" in different times and places) will not serve the narrative poet in his attempt to create characters any better than explanations of hypothetical neural phenomena will serve in place of an objective presentation of thought and emotion.

So it is that Mr. Jeffers' poems tend to be violent but not vivid, contemporary but unreal, elaborately analytical of behavior but lacking in plausible motivation. Although the dominant trends of our scientific age have agreed in denying or ignoring the fact, a sense of the reality of value is at the very core of experience; but value has been explained away in the reality which Mr. Jeffers accepts, along with personality and the soul. And so experienced

9 That this point of view was not a passing fad of the twenties but continues into the present may be seen if one examines Gardner Murphy's *Personality, A Biosocial Approach to Origins and Structure* (New York, 1948) and Henry A. Murray's *Explorations in Personality* (New York, 1947).

values are not in the poems, or are inadequately present, and most of the longer poems finally fail to convey anything, for the outlook which would be conveyed contains a denial of all the values which are the only means by which in poetry it can be conveyed.

4. *"Margrave"*

Many of these generalizations may be illustrated by an analysis of "Margrave," which has the advantage of being both a narrative poem (and so typical of the bulk of Mr. Jeffers' work) and comparatively short. The poem concerns a young man condemned to death for the murder of a child whom he has kidnapped. (Thus when the poem was written it was completely contemporary—and contemporaneity should, according to Mr. Jeffers' theories, add power to the poem.) The young man was preparing for a career in medicine, or, more precisely, in medical research. (Thus again the poem gains power, according to Mr. Jeffers' theories, by being suited to the expression of scientific material by the main character himself.) In addition to the "mental" and physiological reactions of the condemned man in his cell, the poem also treats the behavior of his father and sister. (In this material the usual ingredients of violence and sensationalism are particularly evident.) So the poem has the additional advantage of being typical in substance as well as in form.

Like most of Mr. Jeffers' long poems, it makes a show of complete objectivity. After all, it is supposed to be presenting the really *real* facts behind an act which the untutored masses judge in terms of illusion. But the poem is actually very subjective both in form and in substance.

It opens with the poet himself leaning on a stone parapet and surveying the real world:

> *On the small marble-paved platform*
> *On the turret on the head of the tower,*
> *Watching the night deepen.*
> *I feel the rock-edge of the continent*
> *Reel eastward with me below the broad stars.*
> *I lean on the broad worn stones of the parapet top*
> *And the stones and my hands that touch them reel*
> *eastward.*

Even after this introduction concerned with the poet and his point of view has continued for twelve lines, we are still not yet ready for Margrave and his story. Further background is necessary, further elaboration of the perspective against which the story will be told, so that there will be no danger of our confusing the real and the unreal.

> *The earth was the world and man was its measure,*
> *   but our minds have looked*
> *Through the little mock-dome of heaven the*
> *   telescope-slotted observatory eyeball, there*
> *   space and multitude came in*
> *And the earth is a particle of dust by a sand-grain*
> *   sun, lost in a nameless cove of the shores of a*
> *   continent.*
> *Galaxy on galaxy, innumerable swirls of innumerable*
> *   stars, endured as it were forever and humanity*
> *Came into being, its two or three million years are a*
> *   moment, in a moment it will certainly cease*
> *   out from being*
> *And galaxy on galaxy endure after that as it were*
> *   forever . . . .*

Of all the data of conscious experience and all the prod-

ucts of reason, then, only the facts and theories of astro-
physics are finally real. And this repudiation of most of
experience in favor of a tiny scientific fragment of it is
explicit:

> *Consciousness? The learned astronomer*
> *Analyzing the light of most remote star-swirls*
> *Has found them—or a trick of distance deludes his*
> *   prism—*
> *All at incredible speeds fleeing outwards from ours.*
> *I thought, no doubt they are fleeing the contagion*
> *Of consciousness that infects this corner of space.*

The introduction continues with an inversion of both
Christian and humanistic values, still from the poet's own
point of view:

> *For often I have heard the hard rocks I handled*
> *Groan, because lichen and time and water dissolve*
> *   them,*
> *And they have to travel down the strange falling*
> *   scale*
> *Of soil and plants and the flesh of beasts to become*
> *The bodies of men; they murmur at their fate*
> *In the hollows of windless nights, they'd rather be*
> *   anything*
> *Than human flesh played on by pain and joy,*
> *They pray for annihilation sooner, but annihilation's*
> *Not in the book yet.*

Now we are almost ready for the story of Margrave,
but before we proceed, I should like to comment on this
lengthy introduction. The poem opens with the poet's
personal interpretation of reality, and because of the
nature of the reality, it must be explained rather than

presented. The opening lines explain what are said to be the ultimate facts of experience, the natural processes, the astronomical spectacle. Then the "old" view is summarized and dismissed. The telescope has shown man reality, to his discomfort. Man, the telescope has disclosed, is not the measure, God is not, even the experienced earth itself is not: the mathematical abstractions of astrophysics are. (In other poems and in other portions of this poem the data and theories of other sciences are admitted to the realm of reality, too.) Man's difference from the rocks and stars, which Mr. Jeffers tells us lies in the fact that man is conscious, is unimportant in an expanding universe—unless, fancifully, one conceives it important because the farther stars seem to be receding as the light from them is analyzed in the spectroscope, seem to be "fleeing" consciousness, the contagion.

Since the poem will be chiefly about the consciousness of a condemned man, who, imprisoned, can no longer act but can still think, and since consciousness is unimportant, one cannot, I suppose, expect the poem to contain any significant revelations of anything at all, for Mr. Jeffers' consciousness must be as dubious a product of diseased matter as is that of Margrave. However sympathetic one may be to the point of view which the poet is presenting, one cannot except the poet from his own generalizations. The story of Margrave, one can only conclude from this introduction, will not be interesting or important in itself, but it will be an illustration of the philosophy, a confirmation of the unimportance of consciousness.

After the passage about the "falling scale" by which stone becomes man, the poem turns to the story, though not without one more comment by the poet. These final introductory remarks are interesting for their explicit statement of the purpose of the poem:

> *So, I thought, the rumor*
> *Of human consciousness has gone abroad in*
> *   the world,*
> *The sane uninfected far-outer universes*
> *Flee it in a panic of escape, as men flee the plague*
> *Taking a city: for look at the fruits of consciousness:*
> *As in young Walter Margrave. . . .*

So the body of the poem begins with Margrave trying to arrange his thoughts. With several explanatory interruptions, these thoughts ("They are going to kill the best brain perhaps in the world, That might have made such discoveries in science") and pictures ("He saw clearly in his mind the little Adrenal glands perched on the red-brown kidneys . . .") continue until, after a lapse of months, his father visits him in prison. Then we are given a monologue in which Margrave tells his father what he might do and say to feign madness and thus to avoid the death penalty; the effect of this is somewhat Shakespearean insofar as that is possible with a Hamlet who has not yet come alive for the reader. For though we know this medical student from the inside, since we are given his thoughts and sensations, we do not really know him at all. True, we have been given a kind of motivation: Margrave has kidnapped and murdered a child (it was like pithing a frog, we are told) to get money to continue his medical education. Margrave asks us to consider "What's one child's life Against a career like mine that might have saved Thousands of children?" And we are told that he committed the act "because his glands and his brain have made him act in another than common manner." (One recalls that one cannot say of different ways of acting that they are right or wrong; morals are simply customs, the psychologists and the anthropologists have told Mr. Jeffers and the rest of us.) But this is a parody of motivation: it is the application of a philosophic theory, which seems to be a sort of Nietzschean nihilism, to the case of Margrave. Margrave has simply become the mouthpiece of the sort of confused diabolism one can find in Jack London and Hitler. If this is *really* all there is to the young man, if these are really his only thoughts and sensations, then he is a monster.

But everything else in the poem, particularly the poet's own comments, suggests that the poem is intended as a tragedy. Here is a young man caught in a web of fate; here, symbolically, is all mankind imprisoned and waiting for death, unable to achieve anything but added pain by its peculiarity of consciousness. There seems to me a certain justness and grandeur in this chief symbolic intention of the poem, considered in the abstract. But when we recall the monster or abstraction that Margrave is, when we recall that never for a moment does he engage our interest or sympathy, then we are apt to decide that the figure of mankind as a condemned prisoner, though just and moving when used by a Kafka, is not just here: for mankind is not a criminal monster whether or not it is innately sinful. The difference between an automaton which kills and rationalizes—both in response to glandular secretions and other presumed determinants—and a man who commits murder is enormous, so enormous indeed that the major symbol of the poem is invalid.

Tragedy happens to people, not to monsters. One need not argue the amount of dignity the tragic character must have, the height from which he must fall, or the nature of the tragic flaw.[10] I should be willing for the moment to settle for a tragic character who is simply human and who suffers. Margrave is not human; I cannot judge whether it suffered or not.

But to return. Briefly summarized, the remainder of the poem takes us to Margrave's father, presumably mad, wandering on the seashore accompanied by his unmarried but pregnant daughter; to the prison again, where we are told of Margrave's hanging ("At last the jerked hemp snapped the neck sideways And bruised the cable of nerves that threads the bone rings," etc) and of the "nerves unorganizing themselves" ("then consciousness wandered home from the cell to the molecule . . ."); and finally back once again to the poet himself, who speaks the concluding lines:

> *Here today, gone tomorrow, desperate wee galaxies*
> *Scattering themselves and shining their substance*
> *   away*
> *Like a passionate thought. It is very well ordered.*

Thus the poem ends as it begins, with the stellar galaxies. But if these universes have become, in the perspective of the poem, "desperate" and "wee," then of course even a human Margrave's life and suffering would be no doubt too insignificant to deserve attention.

A few final comments on a poem that declares throughout that its own subject matter is finally unim-

10 See J. W. Krutch's chapter on the impossibility of tragedy in a scientific age, in *The Modern Temper* (New York, 1929).

portant. (Even if Mr. Jeffers had written more disciplined and concentrated verse the poem would still not have lasting interest; for no character who in himself illustrates the belief that values are illusory or purely subjective and consciousness unimportant can be an interesting character.) Margrave's thoughts represent, we are told in the poem, the "fruits of consciousness"; for one in Margrave's situation, thought can lead to no action which will alter what has already been determined. Consciousness, then, is powerless to affect action and so to touch the "real" world of things and behavior; and it is unnatural, a contagion from which the stars flee. How or why, then, it arose, or descended, from the molecules into the cells we are not told. Apparently nature has room within it for the unnatural—which is extra- if not super-naturalism. I shall not dwell on this one philosophical confusion among the many in the poem, but I should like to quote the passage which completes the confusion by suggesting that unnatural consciousness was "required" by the course of things:

> It is likely the enormous
> Beauty of the world requires for completion our
> ghostly increment,
> It has to dream, and dream badly, a moment of its
> night.

Thoughts of the night in which consciousness exists for a moment are so intolerable that when the poet comes to the last days before Margrave's execution, he omits Margrave's thoughts entirely, though we have been told that Margrave's consciousness will be the chief point of the poem.

Margrave's son at this time
Had only four days to wait, but death now appeared
    so dreadful to him that to speak of his thoughts
    and the abject
Horror, would be to insult humanity more than it
    deserves.

Thus the very structure of the poem confesses that finally to grasp the subject in hand is intolerable. It is for this reason that at what should be the climax of the poem, we have a bare summary instead of a presentation. It is for this reason that Mr. Jeffers' other long poems, as I have remarked earlier, tend to go around their subjects without touching them. Language and imagination falter in the attempt to express a conceived reality that is at once all-inclusive and utterly dead, utterly meaningless, and utterly unlike human experience. To deny all human values is to make it perfectly certain that there will be no value in the denial.

5. *What Science Says*

That there are still elements of greatness and moving passages in Mr. Jeffers' work suggests to me an integrity and a power of character in the man which the thinker would deny and the poet is usually unable to express. It seems to me not accidental that Mr. Jeffers has done what is certainly his best, though not his most popular, work in his short lyrics; for in them there is no need to create character or to expound his views fully. When those views are merely reflected in a mood of stoic acceptance of tragic fate, when the confused elements from the thought of Nietzsche and Spengler are not made explicit, but emerge simply as a prophecy of disaster, then Mr. Jeffers can sometimes write memorable poems. Even in such works the technique is undisciplined and uneven, the language insensitive and given to repetition used as a substitute for precision, and the music effective, if at all, only in the large; but there are elements of greatness in the perception of the central issue of our time, in the honest facing of it, and in the complete absorption in the material. But one has to hasten to say that all these fine qualities are in the end insufficient to make a good poem. A poem is a meaningful form. At times Mr. Jeffers' technique is just barely adequate to the expression of moods and visual perceptions in short lyrics; it is never adequate to his larger philosophic intentions, and his views, as I have tried to show, would make impossible the creation of character even if his verse were more' skillful. Reading any large collection of Mr. Jeffers' verse at one time is apt to create an immense effect of repetition and pretentious and often vulgar emptiness.[11]

This again is not to be wondered at. For there seems to be not very much one can do, poetically, with *electrons, molecules,* and *ganglia.* The words have perfectly clear denotations and either, as some argue, no connotations at all, or else the wrong ones for narrative and dramatic poetry. They are not a central part of the experience of anyone but a scientist, and the use to which they are put in Mr. Jeffers' verse denies the importance of all experience, even, finally, the scientific. The impasse is complete.

[11] This effect was confirmed for me after this chapter was written by my reading of *The Double Axe,* Mr. Jeffers' latest volume. Here the vulgarity seems to me complete, the anger sophomoric, the ideas Westbrook Peglerian, the verse utterly inept, and the whole performance beneath critical notice.

What Mr. Jeffers has lately taken to calling his "inhuman-ism" calls for just one thing, silence—as, indeed, Mr. Jeffers has recognized in "Margrave" and elsewhere:

> *I also am not innocent*
> *Of contagion, but have spread my spirit on the*
>   *deep world.*
> *I have gotten sons and sent the fire wider. . . .*
> *And have widened in my idleness*
> *The disastrous personality of life with poems.*

The power and reality which Mr. Jeffers has sought are clearly not the kind of power and reality poetry has and must have. Fact of the kind Mr. Jeffers has used so lavishly in his verse is more effective in the building of a bridge or the performing of a surgical operation than in the building of a poem. And beliefs of the sort that Mr. Jeffers has borrowed from science are chiefly effective in hastening the coming of the "happy hill of not-being," the "confident inorganic glory."

Mr. Jeffers' verse seems to me to confirm Robinson's belief that in a universe of efficient but no final or formal causes, neither poetry nor life itself are finally conceivable. Efficient causes *are* all, says Mr. Jeffers, and the sum of things is beautiful and well ordered, and oblivion is greatly to be desired. If any have supposed that Robinson's fears, Frost's scoffing, and Eliot's disdainful turning of the back on modernism and the implications of science were without any justification, there is the work of Mr. Jeffers, former student of medicine, brother of an astronomer, frequent visitor to observatories, and constant reader of scientific books and journals, to correct them. Mr. Jeffers is in a position to know what the implications of science are for the status of values. I believe a deeper knowledge of modern science and scientific philosophy than most literary critics have would show that he does know, though his information does not seem to be the latest available. He is the only modern poet whose work is widely held to be important who has accepted without any qualification the views of life and man explicitly offered or implicitly suggested by the traditional scientific texts. This at once accounts for his great popularity with the intellectuals of the twenties and thirties—and many still today—and for his larger failures as a poet. His answer to Lord Russell's question is unambiguous: to give up both the aspirations and the poetry in which they have found their expression.

VI. Archibald MacLeish:
The Undigested Mystery

*The poetic form of an age does not reflect the
conditions of the age, political, social, economic;
but the state of its sensibility. And its conception
of man's place in relation to the universe.*
—JOHN PEALE BISHOP *in* "Notes on Obscurity."

1. *An Aspect of Eternity*

Atomistic materialism, though reinvigorated and rede-
fined since the rise of modern science in the Renaissance and especially since the middle of the nineteenth
cntury, is at least as old as Lucretius. Recognition of the
tragic incompleteness and limitation of life, and of justice
as an ideal rather than a fact, and the attempt to accom-
modate oneself to the perceived reality—this is as old as
literature at least. So is the deploring of knowledge without wisdom. Satanism is very old indeed, and in the guise
of nihilistic naturalism may be studied in Hobbes and
Nietzsche.

There is a partially valid point of view, then, from
which one may say that Robinson, Frost, Eliot, and Jeffers
are simply reinterpreting for our day attitudes of great
antiquity. None of them, it may be asserted, has thoroughly assimilated the really new, the distinctively contemporary scientific revelations. For it is not the ideas implied by classical physics or nineteenth-century biology,
it is not the crude materialism of the behaviorists—which,

as an outlook rather than a method, was expressed by Mark Twain and Hobbes among others and implied by the whole course of pre-twentieth-century scientific thought—it is not even the ultimately biological psychology of Freud which most completely distinguishes our age from preceding ages. All these things are further expressions or clarifications of points of view long held or implications long present but not fully recognized. What really distinguishes our age from earlier ones, what keeps it from being but a refinement and development, scientifically, of the age of Herbert Spencer, is what has been called the "sharp turn in the river of knowledge"[1] that began in electro-physics about 1900.[2] With the publication of the Special and later the General theories of relativity, with the rise of quantum physics, with the work of Einstein, Planck, De Broglie, Schrödinger, Heisenberg, and Born, the twentieth century came of age scientifically. The resulting new conception of time and space, the disappearance of scientific authority for any conception of the universe which could be represented by a mechanical model, the realization that "matter" and "energy" are interchangeable variants of the same mysterious force—these constitute the great advances of contemporary science.

But before the work of Archibald MacLeish in the late nineteen twenties and early nineteen thirties, they had not significantly informed modern poetry. And what Mr. MacLeish did with this new information and these new

[1] So called by Sir James Jeans in *The Mysterious Universe* (New York, 1933).

[2] For an excellent layman's summary of the achievements and significance of the revolution in physics, see Lincoln Barnett, *The Universe and Dr. Einstein* (New York, 1949).

attitudes was not simply to write poetry *about* relativity and the new dissolution of the solid world, though he did that, too: he assimilated the new doctrines early and emerged with a sensibility partly formed by influences that had not existed a generation before, a sensibility, aspects of which have since become characteristic of those who are really contemporary with Einstein and White-head.

Newness is, of course, a relative concept, but the sense of time and space and time-space, the "sense of infinity," that informs Mr. MacLeish's early work was perhaps as new as anything in poetry ever is. For Bruno the sense of physical infinity was a concomitant of his faith in the infinitude of mind; for Spinoza the effort to see things *sub specie aeternitatis* was conditioned by an unquestioning acceptance of the world as a rational order. For Mr. Mac-Leish the sense of infinity is first of all physical, an awareness of time, of space, of man's position on the planet; and then, since man is a spirit as well as a creature, it is a sense both human and spiritual. For by an easy symbolic transformation the physical facts of man's position on the planet and his motion through space may be transformed into spiritual facts. Religion starts with a spiritual awareness and works in the opposite direction; the process is reversible. Theologians have recognized general as well as special revelation. One notes that historic Christianity and Mr. MacLeish end not far apart on man's situation. Despite Mr. Eliot's condescension toward the great contemporary physicists and Mr. Frost's denial that the size of the universe has anything to do with man's destiny, one may, as the poetry of Mr. MacLeish testifies, start one's attempt to see things under the aspect of eternity by trying imaginatively to realize the significance of astrophysics.

2. *The Sense of Infinity and the Unanswered Question*

The distinguishing feature of much of Mr. MacLeish's best work, of nearly all of that written before 1933, is his sense of man's physical situation in cosmic space. The restless motion of the sea is everywhere, and man is a "seafarer":

> *And learn O voyager to walk*
> *The roll of earth, the pitch and fall*
> *That swings across these trees those stars:*
> *That swings the sunlight up the wall.*

The early poems are full of "the rushing sound the planet makes"; and his sense of this sound makes the poet declare that he has "the sense of infinity." And that this sensibility is related to the new physics is everywhere clear; quite apart from the poem on Einstein there are frequent allusions to concepts that are utterly at variance with the conceptions of classical physics.[3] Although the reference to the "dead planet" in "Cinema of Man" may suggest Tennyson or Robinson, such an allusion as that to a universe finite but unbounded in "Lines for a Prologue" is unlike anything in older poetry. (With the old mysteries supposedly dissipated, we create new ones: how shall one understand "finite but unbounded"?)

Contemporary physics is not concerned with attempting to "picture" an atom; indeed it warns that we must

[3] The most succinct definition of the physical universe as it is revealed by modern science is that it is *a four-dimensional space-time continuum.*

not try to do so. But one of its fundamental conceptions is that this basic unit of the once solid world is overwhelmingly "empty space." The microscopic turns out, then, to resemble the macroscopic in this all-important respect. Only in the world of ordinary sense experience is there density, solidity, stability. That is why some have felt that contemporary physics substantiates philosophic idealism, Platonic or otherwise. Mr. MacLeish draws no such conclusion, but his poems are dominated by an awareness of space, not of matter, and the reality they suggest is as fluid and insubstantial as may well be within the limitations imposed by the necessity of using symbols drawn from sense experience.

Mr. MacLeish's problem as a poet, then, has been to translate conceptions essentially unpicturable into terms of sense, to turn a physics become almost completely mathematical into poetry. "A wave has broken in the sea beyond the coast of Spain." Physical images succeed, in the best poems, in evoking a world no longer closed and solid. One seems to see, to feel, all around it, beyond it, even through it. Around the rushing planet "the unknown constellations sway." Thus when Mr. MacLeish came to compose an epitaph he composed it around the idea of the earth's motion; movement in space is the object of contemplation in "Immortal Helix":

Hereunder Jacob Schmidt who, man and bones,
Has been his hundred times around the sun.

His chronicle is endless—the great curve
Inscribed in nothing by a point upon
The spinning surface of a spinning sphere.

Dead bones roll on.

So also in the poem on Shakespeare, "Verses for a Centennial," it is a sense of the *spot* where the poet was buried that controls the other attitudes in the poem: in a world of universal relative motion in space-time, the marbles of the illustrious dead are forever lost:

> *Where now, where now along the great ecliptic*
> *Traced by a wandering planet that unwinds*   .
> *Space into hours?*

In such a world the bones of the dead find no rest and the living can discover even in thought no fixed point of reference. In Mr. MacLeish's rewriting of Mother Goose we "die of vertigo" induced by the universal spinning. With the disappearance of Newton's absolute space and the nineteenth century's refuge from mystery, the ether, the last conceptual shield against the sound of "the surf that breaks upon Nothing" has gone.[4] As the nineteenth century dissolved man into his physics and chemistry, so Einstein has dissolved the world into a set of mathematical equations.[5] Those who long for something

[4] "But the deeper science probes toward reality, the more clearly it appears that the universe is not like a machine at all." (Barnett, *The Universe and Dr. Einstein*, 78) "Space and time have vanished into the merest shadows, and only a sort of combination of the two preserves any reality." (Herman Minkowski, quoted in Barnett, *ibid.*, 64.) This evaporation of the solid, machinelike, and so picturable universe is the conclusion drawn by all the major interpreters of science with whose works I am acquainted; yet, because it seems to some to open the door to religious speculations, it is often implicitly or explicitly denied; and Einstein, Eddington, Jeans, Weyl, and the other major scientists who emphasize the point are stigmatized and dismissed as "religious scientists."

[5] "But the paradox of physics today is that with every improvement in its mathematical apparatus the gulf between the observer and the objective world of scientific description becomes more profound." (Barnett, *ibid.*, 14.) The mathematics of modern physics implies a cosmology, it is true, but the cosmos implied is difficult to conceive and impossible to picture. Hart Crane tried to suggest it in his poetry, with what success

more ultimate than a frame of reference may feel as little at ease in the Einsteinian world as in the Newtonian. The dominant emotion in Mr. MacLeish's early work is a sense of unease, of homelessness, which wavers between anxiety and nostalgia. Although the implications of the new science are held by most philosophers to be less contradictory to the assumptions of both humanism and religion than those of the old science, yet the old awareness of mortality has been stimulated anew, for now everything, even geometry, is a reminder of time and death. In a world in which time is a function of space, says Mr. MacLeish, one can *feel* the "always coming on of night." To feel it thus, geometrically, astronomically, spatially, is to feel it in the peculiarly twentieth-century way. It is, in fact, to translate Relativity into poetry.

In such a world as we now conceive, these poems say, men are afraid. Of primitive peoples the poet says in "Land's End":

> *They are not afraid as we are here*
> *For they know what the world is.*

The woman in "Selene Afterwards" is afraid of something undefined, "as though the plunge of space Over the world's rim frightened her." We have discovered new emotional reasons for our terror:

each must judge for himself. As Sir Arthur S. Eddington said some years ago, "The conceptions of physics are becoming difficult to understand. First relativity theory, then quantum theory and wave mechanics have transformed the universe, making it seem fantastic to our minds. . . . But there is another side to the transformation. Naïve realism, materialism, and mechanistic conceptions of phenomena were simple to understand; but I think that it was only by closing our eyes to the essential nature of conscious experience that they could be made to seem credible." (*New Pathways in Science* [New York, 1935], 91.)

It was a woman's skull the shriveling cold
Out there among the stars had withered dry.

In such a world man is both everything and nothing. He tries to think, but he can think only of the way "this world against the wind of time Perpetually falls." Attempting to hold fast to the sensed reality of people, he finds that they, too, have been dissolved into geometrical relations:

These live people,
These more
Than three dimensional
By time protracted edgwise into heretofore
People.

"Signature for Tempo" marks the entry into modern poetry of a full realization of space-time, the four dimensional world. Here is the essence of the new vision of our century. In such a world what questions may we ask and what answers expect?

3. *Were There Not Words?*

In "Reproach to Dead Poets" Mr. MacLeish contrasts the confident articulateness of the poets of earlier ages with the inarticulateness of poets of our day. Poets once had the words for what they wanted to say, but poets today cannot use the old words and they have found no substitutes for them. One thinks of Mr. Eliot's comments on words in *Four Quartets,* and one recalls that as beliefs decay the words that denote them are lost or altered. Dead poets lived in an orderly and understandable world, and their poetry could partake of that order and luminosity. Like the waiter in Hemingway's great story, poets today long for a clean, well-lighted place. "Men of my century loved Mozart," says Mr. MacLeish: loved him because his music has order, pattern, perfect articulateness. Behind our discovery of pre-Romantic music lies nostalgia for a simpler, less mysterious, more rational and human world.

With that world gone, Mr. MacLeish has made what is left do. With the beliefs gone that once served poets, both as poets and as men as well, there are left the facts, theories, and hypotheses of science; these must serve. Yeats fabricated a mythology of his own; Mr. Eliot became a Christian. But Mr. MacLeish, neither myth-maker nor traditionalist, has written many poems out of a generalized anxiety and the data and implications of recent science. That fact no doubt has something to do with both the originality and the increasingly evident weaknesses of his work, perhaps also with his tendency in the last decade or so to turn from poetry to prose. His best work was done after his earliest experimentation and before his turn to the writing of radio drama and prose; it is all in the volume *Poems, 1924–1933*. And some of the best things in the book are as much "the poetry of science" as is the work of Mr. Jeffers, though the science that is used is very different.

"The Hamlet of A. MacLeish," for example, turns the ghost of Hamlet's father into the ghostly physical world of modern knowledge. When men turn their eyes to "that vast silence overhead" and question it, there is no sound. The stars they seem to see shining may be dark by "now," for the light that reaches their eyes started on its journey long ago. But there is no *now*, so that questions of time and eternity cannot even be formulated.

No ghost of any kind was ever harder to question than the world inhabited by the modern Hamlet. When the marginal notes read, "The King his father's ghost appears to him," the verse reads,

> *At night the sky*
> *Opens, the near things vanish, the bright walls*
> *Fall, and the stars were always there, and the dark*
> *There and the cold and the stillness.*

At one point Hamlet suggests that there is a reason for the confused and helpless state of his feelings:

> *I have heard from the ancient*
> *Westward greying face of the wandering planet*
> *The voices calling the small new name of god.*

And it is clear that it is Hamlet's realization that "we are alone upon this place," alone with "the vacant light, The bright void, the listening, idiot silence" that prevents him from acting or even thinking fruitfully or consecutively. Mr. MacLeish's Hamlet is at once a more articulate and explicit and a less distinctly conceived Prufrock. As Prufrock is unable to bring himself to the point of putting the question, so Hamlet in his confusion and paralysis of understanding knows only that

> *We have learned the answers, all the answers:*
> *It is the question that we do not know.*

Yet there is a question implied throughout the poem, and it is the question which Robinson asked. (Symbolist and modern, Mr. MacLeish cannot use words like *Purpose* and *Law,* which Robinson was able to use without embarrassment; but the question is there.) No answer comes, but the silence itself is sufficient answer. The poem's frequent echoes of Mr. Eliot are all of that aspect of Mr. Eliot's work which seemed to critics of the twenties to make him one of the "lost generation." Again, the emotions Hamlet is made to feel are much like those urbanely dissected by Henry Adams a generation before. The answer to the unarticulated question is clear enough.

"The Hamlet" is one of Mr. MacLeish's very early poems. More mature and, despite the popularity of Hamlet's attitudes during the twenties, more distinctly contemporary, is the very fine "You, Andrew Marvell." Completely dominated by the distinguishing feature of Mr. MacLeish's sensibility, his sense of time and space, it demonstrates among other things that there is a more fruitful way for science to make itself felt in poetry than Mr. Jeffers' discursive use of scientific terms and theories. Here the data of astronomy have been transmuted and what has emerged is a new sensibility. The unity of time and space, the sensory infinitude of the Heraclitean flux, are really grasped in this tribute to a poet rediscovered by a generation in search of a tradition adequate to its experience. Unlike "The Hamlet," the poem has an organic structure and a simple theme: the poem shows us what it is like

> *To feel the always coming on*
> *The always rising of the night.*

Certainly the poem, if not the best, is one of the several best Mr. MacLeish has ever written; and its distinctive feature is its expression of temporal meanings by the use of spatial symbols.

"Einstein" is not only the finest poetic tribute to the scientist, it is also an informed and interesting comment

on the philosophical significance of Einstein's achievement. The chief idea to emerge from the poem is that
the new Einsteinian science has at once emphasized the
centrality and increased the loneliness of the knowing
mind. As Hamlet found that his attempt to formulate
questions of meaning were discouraged by the idiot silence, so the Einstein of the poem, having dissolved the
external world into a set of mental calculations, can come
in contact with nothing outside himself, can in fact not
even penetrate imaginatively the surrounding emptiness.
He is left with his own awareness as the only indisputable
reality. The "something inviolable" which begins and
ends the poem, though it suggests that an assertion of
faith is being made, particularly if one contrasts it with
the denial of spirit made by the philosophical behaviorists, implies a grim sort of solipsism rather than religious
or philosophical faith in order or meaning. Spirit seems
to me to be as lost, and nearly as helpless, in Mr. Mac-
Leish's version of an Einsteinian world as it is in Mr.
Jeffers' pre-Einsteinian one.

Again it is the sense of our astronomical position that
distinguishes the poem. Again, as in "The Hamlet," the
structure is external, Einstein's unmotivated actions serv-
ing as a frame on which are strung the speculations and
sentiments which make up the poem. Unlike that of
"You, Andrew Marvell," however, the perspective here
is geometrical rather than geographical, though in the
end the two come to the same thing, a sense of space.
Here we have the geometry of man in an equational
world. Like the cubist, Mr. MacLeish reduces experience
to "perpendiculars and curves and planes"; when this
reduction threatens to dissolve consciousness itself, Ein-

stein and the poet together reject it and keep "something inviolate. A living something."

But though he thus refuses to eliminate mind from reality, Einstein still finds himself lost in the world which he has constructed. Though "suddenly he feels The planet plunge beneath him," though he sees the "awful shadows loom across the sky That have no life from him," though, in short, astronomical and physical concepts have become so familiar to him that they seem to be sensed rather than known, still the world of science and the world of experience draw farther and farther apart.[6]

> *Although they seize*
> *His sense, he has no name for them, no word*
> *To give them meaning and no utterance*
> *For what they say.*

The "childhood home" has been lost with the "lost youth." The mind which has penetrated the secret places finds at last one place impenetrable. Repulsed there, it feels itself being dissolved into molecules, itself reduced to the forces which it has calculated, become merely a spot in space. When finally it succeeds in entering by the Back Stair, it resists dissolution but is equally resisted by the secret:

> *Like a foam*
> *His flesh is withered and his shriveling*
> *And ashy bones are scattered on the dark.*
> *But still the dark denies him. Still withstands*
> *The dust his penetration and flings back*
> *Himself to answer him. Which seems to keep*
> *Something inviolate. A living something.*

[6] See the Introduction to Eddington's *The Nature of the Physical World* (New York, 1931).

Despite, then, its *Cogito, ergo sum* affirmation, the poem expresses the sense of isolation and alienation which haunts modern man. Its affirmation is minimal and desperate.

"Epistle To Be Left in the Earth" contains the essence of what Mr. MacLeish believed his generation had discovered about the world. And only fools and philistines will deny the permanent validity of many of the insights of the MacLeish-Hemingway generation. The poem is a summary of our discoveries left for the enlightenment of any who may come after man has disappeared. (Here Mr. MacLeish and Mr. Jeffers find themselves on common ground.) Its form is that of the broken and incoherent phrase in loose free verse, so that it gives one the impression of reading an only partly decipherable letter in a strange tongue, a letter, too, written under great duress, like the messages written by the last to die of lost Arctic expeditions. It begins with the coming of death— ". . . It is colder now"—and ends with an assertion of ignorance —"Voices are crying an unknown name in the sky." Between death and ignorance, the poem says, lie all the experiences and all the certainties of a generation.

One notes that the lines that follow the opening "It is colder now" evoke an astronomical perspective. This is the perspective which controls the meaning of the ordinary phenomena of earth that follow—leaves falling, water, jays, crows; and it is in this perspective that man must evaluate his beliefs and uncertainties:

> *Each man believes in his heart he will die*
> *Many have written last thoughts and last letters*
> *None know if our deaths are now or forever*
> *None know if this wandering earth will be found.*

146

When the poem comes to the heart of the message ("I will tell you all we have learned"), we find the astronomical perspective re-emphasized: the first of all the facts we have learned is that the earth is round. (We tend to forget, so familiar are we with it, that this is not a sensed datum but a deduction.) Then, after fragments of sense experience and folklore presented as though they constituted all our wisdom and were equal in importance among themselves, we come to a conclusion in which things of sense and things of thought are jumbled in a symbolic assertion of mingled ignorance and fear:

> *Also none among us has seen God*
> *(. . . We have thought often*
> *The flaws of sun in the late and driving weather*
> *Pointed to one tree but it was not so)*
> *As for the nights I warn you the nights are dangerous*
> *The wind changes at night and the dreams come*
>
> *It is very cold*
>
>   *there are strange stars near Arcturus*
>
> *Voices are crying an unknown name in the sky.*

Thus a poem which begins with cold which it equates with the cold and lifelessness of interstellar space[7] ends with cold first sensed and then conceived and with mystery first conceived and then sensed. Thought and sense have worked together in the poem to produce an overwhelming feeling of alienation. Mr. MacLeish has here

[7] One might add—and this is included in the meaning of the poem—that the cold and the lifelessness are, according to evidence afforded by modern physical science, not only interstellar but ultimate: they are the conditions toward which all sensible nature is approaching, the conditions summarized in scientific terms as "heat-death" or "maximum entropy."

done in permanently interesting verse what Mr. Hemingway has done so magnificently in prose.

"Conquistador" is a very different sort of poem—and
it seems to me not nearly so successful—but it is dominated by the same emotions and the same items of awareness. Its piled-up fragments of sense experience and factual memories, its blood and girls and comrades, its dust
and names of towns, the repetition and irrelevance which
are the essence of its structure—all of its form and all
of its substance are the product of attitudes which I have
already examined as they appear in other poems. The
sense which informs it all is a sense of

> *Dust under the whistling of hawks!*
> *Companion of*
> *Constellations the trace of his track lies!*
> *Endless is the unknown earth before a man . . . .*

"Conquistador" is another epistle to be left in the earth,
another record of man as seafarer, another revelation of
the nothing, nothing at all outside the big top.

The surface intention of the form of the poem is that
of producing the effect of reading the old records, particularly the book by Bernal Díaz cited in the introductory note. Thus the first aim is a kind of historical verisimilitude. But "history" has many meanings and many
ambiguities. Here the past is remembered, not interpreted, and the memories are those of an old man approaching death. The fragmentation, then, the irrelevance, the unpredictable and inconsequent vividness
alternating with dry facts and meaningless names are all
consistent with the surface intention of the poem; and
those critics who have condemned the work as inadequate

history are missing the point, for the aim is not history as of the history books, but history as remembered experience. (The critics might also have remembered that this is poetry, whether it is successful or not, and that it can hardly be judged by the criteria one would apply to a book by Charles Beard.) A soldier's memories of a war in which he has fought are naturally quite different from a historian's summary and interpretation. If the poem achieves the kind of personal, subjective, historical verisimilitude it obviously aimed at, then it is a successful poem on this level. And the poem is vivid with sense experience in many parts, though there is much too much of it; and the past has been imaginatively recovered. The poem is successful as history—as its kind of history.

But to justify its structure and substance on this level is to condemn it; for the poem clearly aims at being more than a poetic translation of historical records. The narrative of the conquerors is a parable: like the conquerors of Mexico, we engage in an enterprise, the purpose of which is forgotten as we proceed through a land always strange and filled with unknown horrors, fighting the same battles again and again, assailed by sense and filled with nostalgia and weariness, fearful but still driven by unsatisfied desire. The land of the conquerors is as much a waste land as the London of Mr. Eliot. The exoticism of the landscape is superficial: here are the same "strained time-ridden faces Distracted from distraction by distraction," the endless motion in a circle, the shadowy forms whom death has undone. Here there is motion without direction, passion without purpose, sensation without meaning. Nothing but the surface of "Conquistador" is alien to contemporary experience. But as a parable expressive of an indictment of contemporary life, the poem is only partially successful. It seems too much, when one reflects upon it, the product of a mood, too little the product of a judgment. For if it is a judgment, by what standard is the judgment made? The religious standards of Mr. Eliot, the humanistic ones of Mr. Frost, the anti-human ones of Mr. Jeffers—all standards by which experience may be evaluated are here lacking. What remains, then, is only weariness and the most elementary sort of judgment: we recognize the waste land, but do not know why it is familiar until we recall *The Waste Land* and *The Modern Temper*.

There are, of course, other reasons why the poem is not successful. The poem lacks density of texture and interest of structure. To have been successful as a parable, it should have been either recognizably particularized in the manner of *Gulliver's Travels* or based on archetypal myths in the manner of *The Waste Land;* the first way might have served as well as the second. Again, and more important, lacking a sure sense of structure, the poet depended too much on the old records and ended by producing a poem faithful even to their tediousness. Perhaps one conclusion to be drawn is that if one wants to picture a world without meaning, narrating in detail the meaningless actions of tired men is not the best way to go about it. Or again, more seriously, one must certainly conclude that Mr. MacLeish's artistry has sometimes not been adequate to his sensibility. But even if his artistry had been surer in "Conquistador," there are limits to what one can see from the vantage point of the poet at the time when he wrote the poem. This seems to me the most significant consideration of all: for the sensibility

here is the same as that in "You, Andrew Marvell"; yet
in the lyric it seems perfectly adequate, here utterly inadequate. Man's physical situation in his astronomical
setting is one thing; his life, however, is more than physical and must be judged by standards and seen from perspectives more complicated than the astronomical. Precisely because "Conquistador" is about the whole life of
man, it fails. For the most part the poem seems to move
as the conquerors sometimes marched, "By night, by
darkness, turning from the sun."

4. *An Image of the World*

When in the late thirties Mr. MacLeish called for an
image of the world in which men could again believe,
he was calling for something which is absent from his own
best poetry, as he himself seems to have realized. The
"image" which dominates the poetry written before Mr.
MacLeish turned to writing poems of social conscience
and current topics in the mid-thirties is an image of a
shadowy something—which we must still call by its old
and misleading name, matter—in motion in space-time.
The illumination it gives to the nature of man and his
place in the cosmos is no *ignis fatuus,* but it occupies only
a narrow band in the spectrum. That, it seems to me, is
one of the reasons why "The End of the World" and
"You, Andrew Marvell" are fine poems, but "Conquistador" is only an interesting failure. Like ultraviolet
light, the light cast by Mr. MacLeish's image of the world
is useless for seeing one's way around but useful for de-
stroying diseases to which man is subject—pride and a
false sense of security, for instance. The vision of reality

found in Mr. MacLeish's poems is like a part of the vision of historic Christianity[8] in that it is calculated to destroy man's pretensions—those of philosophic idealism and those of rationalism, those of scientific positivism and those of bourgeois optimism equally. And it does so in somewhat the same fashion, by enlarging man's perspective more than it is comfortable to have it enlarged. A firm imaginative grasp of the realities of time and space is incompatible with complacency.

But after the pretensions are destroyed, a new and more subtly grounded, a more intelligent, a wiser confidence must be gained or we have nihilism or quietism. So it was that in 1931 Mr. MacLeish wrote that poetry, "which owes no man anything, owes nevertheless one debt—an image of the world in which men can again believe."[9] (The belief that poetry should thus fulfill the role of philosophy and religion is one of the more curious of our inheritances from Victorianism.) For as Mr. MacLeish wrote later, "No purposed human action is conceivable without an image of the world which is coherent and distinguishable."[10] The image which Mr. MacLeish wants is one which would allow his Einstein to penetrate and not to be repulsed, to grasp something real and solid outside his own consciousness which would yet not be a contradiction of the reality of that consciousness, which would give the conquerors something besides the blood and the girls to remember and to be guided by, which would bring some order out of the chaotic fragments

[8] See, for example, Reinhold Niebuhr, *The Nature and Destiny of Man* (one-volume edition, New York, 1948).

[9] "Nevertheless One Debt," *Poetry*, Vol. XXXVIII (July, 1931), 216.

[10] "The American Writer and the New World," *Yale Review*, Vol. XXXI, No. 1 (Autumn, 1941), 77.

which so aptly suggest the fragmentation and alienation of the modern mind in "Epistle To Be Left in the Earth." Such an image need not contradict, though it will certainly supplement, the insights into man's position in space that give interest and value to Mr. MacLeish's best poems. Ten years ago, in his denunciation of the "irresponsibles" of his own generation, Mr. MacLeish asserted his faith in "moral law," in "spiritual authority," and in "intellectual truth." There is nothing in Einsteinian science, though there is much in the spirit of our age, which makes such a faith impossible to formulate or to recover.

And there is nothing in Mr. MacLeish's poems, even in the earliest, which forbids or denies it, though the emphasis is elsewhere. From the very beginning, as I have tried to show, it is the effect of strictly contemporary, not of late Victorian, science that is apparent in the poems. There is no old-fashioned materialism or mechanism present. Physics and astro-physics, which are at once the oldest sciences, the ones whose results are most certain, and the furthest advanced, have had a greater influence in the shaping of the poet's sensibility than any of the other sciences; and even if we utterly discount the testimony of the religious scientists, as I should not object to doing, since achievement in science does not in itself qualify a man as a philosopher, we may still say with complete certainty that there is nothing in recent physical science which logically discourages belief in the objectivity of value. (The implications of classical physics did conflict, or seem to conflict, with belief in the objectivity of value; the roots of the science-religion controversy of the nineteenth century went far deeper than the reconcilers of Darwin and Genesis realized.)

Mr. MacLeish's development, then, does not represent an about-face, as some have suggested, a change from a man of the lost generation to a man of faith (or a man who wishes he had faith). Which is not to say that his development has nothing in common with the developments of Aldous Huxley, Ernest Hemingway, W. H. Auden, and all the rest. Rather, it is to say that each of these began with something which he had later to cast off, to deny; while Mr. MacLeish began with a sensibility which needed only to be supplemented by the new image which he desires. It is perhaps not too far-fetched to suggest that his devotion to social themes during the thirties and his comparative silence since, even perhaps what seems like the deterioration of his poetic powers—that these may all have something to do with his failure to find any ground for the new image more secure than the will to believe.

The will to believe is certainly present, but so also are the vacant light, the bright void, the listening, idiot silence. The "undigested mystery" remains undigested. Mystery there will always be, certainly, but it seems to me that the poet, if not the man, must somehow manage to digest it.

VII. Hart Crane: Beyond All Sesames of Science

For, after all, look and see how roundly the world has of late been disabused of the most and the best of its myths—and as a consequence has been stricken with an unheard of poverty of mind and unhappiness of life.—JOHN CROWE RANSOM *in* God Without Thunder.

1. *My Hand in Yours*

I suppose no poet has ever set for his accomplishment a more ambitious project than did Hart Crane. And perhaps none in our time has failed more gloriously. For he did fail: his myth refused to crystalize into coherent and significant form; even he did not, in the end, believe in it. Yet in the process of trying to forge a myth which would be a passage to India for his generation, he wrote some of the finest poetry of the century.

Nothing, it has long been conceded, is easier for the critic than to show how the more ambitious poems of gifted poets fail in one way or another. And the activity is pleasurable as well as easy: one's gifts seem to increase as one points out the mistakes of the gifted. The Augustans have said enough on this so that no more need be said, except by way of particularization: one may concentrate on either Hart Crane's great achievements or his outstanding failure without departing from the facts of his work. Mr. Winters has shown us how Crane inherited

155

and magnified the errors of romantic religious naturalism, and Mr. Brom Weber has recently diagnosed the poet as a borderline psychotic. Both profess admiration for certain passages and poems, yet both demolish the intention and achievement of *The Bridge* and end by considerably lessening the poet's stature, the one by reducing him to an object-lesson in philosophical error, the other by making us wonder how so mad a man produced such fine poems and by treating religious poetry from a materialistic standpoint.[1] Yet if *The Bridge* manifestly fails of its intention, it also contains the poet's finest poetry, not simply in isolated lines but in long passages and whole sections. There must have been something about the design of *The Bridge* which called forth Crane's finest powers, yet left him helpless to achieve his aim.

Crane explained his design at length—at rather too great length, I think—to Otto Kahn, who was subsidizing him, to his friends, to anyone who would listen or write him a letter in return. (One of the troubles with Mr. Weber's book is that he takes the ideas Crane expressed in his prose a little too seriously, the achieved content of the poems not quite seriously enough. Crane found nothing easier than to project plans for poems, to outline the profound symbolic significance they would have, to "ex-

---

[1] The first in "Primitivism and Decadence" and "The Significance of The Bridge," both available in *In Defense of Reason* (New York, 1947); the second in *Hart Crane* (New York, 1948). I myself have added to the extensive literature analyzing Crane's failure in two essays which I have come partially to regret, though most of their content still seems to me true: "Hart Crane's Bridge to Cathay," *American Literature*, Vol. XVI, No. 2 (May, 1944), 115–30; and "Hart Crane and the Broken Parabola," *The University of Kansas City Review*, Vol. XI, No. 3 (Spring, 1945), 173–77.

plain" his work, both written and projected, in terms which he manifestly only partly understood. He was, of course, prompted to do this during the composition of *The Bridge* by his need to justify himself to Mr. Kahn, who was advancing money without seeing any results, and to himself; but it was his nature to do it anyway.) Crane's ideas were not much more stable than his emotions. His violent changes from exaltation to depression, from belief to skepticism, from an idea to its contrary— in short, his mental instability and confusion force one to take his statements of intention and belief with the greatest caution, to look for trends of opinion rather than any final clarification of what he thought he was about.

But concerning the over-all intention of *The Bridge* a few things are certain. Taking Whitman as his model, he wanted to fashion a myth for his day which would "synthesize" the discordant elements in American experience. As Whitman had praised "the strong light works of engineers" but had seen these as preliminary to and symbolic of achievements in spiritual growth; as Whitman had reconciled science and religion, materialism and faith; as Whitman had bridged the gap between East and West and proclaimed the oneness of the world and the brotherhood of man—so Crane's bridge was to join the bipolarities of modern America in a synthesis at once mystical and historical. Despite Crane's enormous debt to Eliot, a debt which has not been sufficiently recognized, the poem which more than any other suggests the intended meaning of *The Bridge* is Whitman's "Passage to India." Although it is one of the most seriously flawed sections of Crane's poem, "Cape Hatteras," which reaffirms Whitman's vision and culminates in an invocation of Whitman's spirit, is the chief internal clue to the meaning of *The Bridge*. It clarifies the intention—by setting it in a framework—of such general statements of Crane's as that the poem was to celebrate man's "conquest of space and knowledge,"[2] that his concern as a poet was with the "articulation of contemporary human consciousness," and that his aim was to create an "integration of experience."[3]

When he said in his essay "Modern Poetry" that Whitman seemed to him "the most typical and valid expression of the American psychosis," he revealed both one of his few unwavering opinions and his inadequate education. (Why *psychosis?* Did he really consider the American character not simply neurotic but *psychotic?* And if so, how did this fit with his intention of celebrating American character and achievement in *The Bridge?* But it is more likely that Crane did not really know the meaning of the word, that he was confusing it with *psyche,* using it as a more impressive variant of *temperament* or *soul.* The point is not a minor one: such ignorance or confusion or both are everywhere in Crane except in his best poetry; and his ignorance has something to do with his failure in *The Bridge* to articulate a valid myth or even to create a poem with a coherent and sensible prose meaning.) Canal and bridge, railroad and airplane, India and Cathay—these are the symbols which declare the practical identity of purpose of the two poets. "My hand in yours, Walt Whitman, so . . ."

2 Weber, *Hart Crane,* 258.

3 "Modern Poetry," Crane's poetic credo, in *The Collected Poems of Hart Crane,* ed. by Waldo Frank (New York, 1933).

2. *The Logic of Ecstasy*

One need not share Whitman's and Crane's mystical pantheism in order to acknowledge that their aim was lofty. One need not believe that a religious myth for our time must be created, not rediscovered; or that the first step in its creation must be the "affirmation" of the sum total of the American past and present, the second a "transcending" of these facts; or that man's increasing technological mastery over nature is a good symbol of his increasing spiritual health and closeness to God—one need not agree with these ideas or share these attitudes in order to believe that the subject of *The Bridge* was the most important that can well be imagined, and that the insight that prompted Crane to undertake the poem was an act of genius. One may disagree thus with Crane's ideas, recognize the magnitude and significance of his attempt and the amount of genius that went into the imperfect execution of it, and yet not be in the muddled position which Mr. Winters ascribes to "Professor X." (Mr. Winters' ideas are clear, but clear ideas are not enough.)

For it is possible to show that even if one temporarily suspends judgment of the philosophic validity of Crane's outlook, granting to that outlook perhaps more clarity and consistency than it actually had and ignoring for the moment what Mr. Winters sees as its suicidal implications, still Crane's preparation as well as his temperament made it highly unlikely that he would succeed as a philosophic poet, one who would forge a new myth that would synthesize America's past and its present, fact and ideal, science and religion, man and God.

Crane began as an imagist. He began, that is, as an apprentice in the first American school to rediscover Poe's "heresy of the didactic." Under the tutelage of Mr. Eliot (Crane said that he read *The Waste Land* twenty times) and especially of the little magazines, which were more truly his Harvard and his Yale than ever a whaling ship was Melville's, he quickly moved beyond imagism to symbolism. He began to look into the French symbolists, Rimbaud in particular. But he could not read French, could read no foreign language in fact; and his dictionary and translation labors with the French poets succeeded only in giving him an impression of the strangeness and richness of their texture and the general nature of their procedure. In the end he had to rely on Mr. Eliot and the little magazines for what knowledge he had of poetry outside English—and for his reactions to much within it.

With Mr. Eliot and Ezra Pound he discovered the virtues of the late-nineteenth-century aesthetes and decadents, wrote appreciatively of Oscar Wilde, entitled one of his poems "C33" (Wilde's prison number), and learned to scorn more knowingly the heresy of the didactic. From Mr. Eliot's early criticism he learned that a true poet never thinks, that good poetry is distinguished from bad by the "precision" of its *emotion*. From Mr. Richards, whose *Principles of Literary Criticism* he called in 1927 "a *great* book. One of the few—perhaps the only one in English excepting stray remarks by Coleridge—that get to bed rock,"[4] he learned that our scientific age demands the separation of poetic truth and scientific truth. Mr. Richards had settled the matter:[5] poetry dealt in

4 Weber, *Hart Crane*, 271.
5 In view of my summary dismissal of the early theories of Mr. Rich-

"emotive," science in referential statements. Poetry not only need not, but positively should not, "make sense" in the way prose does. ("We need a spell of purer poetry," advised Mr. Richards.) And Crane's philosophical reading seemed to corroborate this aesthetic doctrine: P. D. Ouspensky, who influenced him more than any other philosopher of the several with whom Crane was familiar, advised the cultivation of a mystical "logic of ecstasy,"[6] a term and a concept which Crane found very easy to identify with the "emotive" language and the "precise emotions" which he had come to look for in poetry.

The identification of Ouspensky's mystical and Richards' positivistic descriptions of poetic logic was essential to Crane. For as he approached the composition of *The Bridge,* he was, as we have seen, becoming convinced that the greatest of tasks for the poet of his day was to "perform anew" Whitman's achievement of a synthesis of science and faith. But it is apparent that if poetry deals only in emotion and leaves truth to science (as Mr. Richards had conceived the matter), it can never "synthesize" conflicting bodies of fact and doctrine. (Mr. Richards had said that the practical value of poetry lay in its function of "ordering" the emotions and attitudes, defining the latter in behavioristic terms.) But Ouspensky had urged the logic of ecstasy as a way to truth wholly superior to that of ordinary logic. Thus by only slightly confusing the

ards, it is interesting to note that even his former student and great admirer William Empson has decided that either the early Richards views of language and poetry were wrong or that Richards did not mean what he seemed to be saying. See "Emotions in Words Again," *Kenyon Review,* Vol. X, No. 4 (Autumn, 1948), 579–601.

6 *Tertium Organum: A Key to the Mysteries of the World* (New York, 1922).

various senses of the words *truth* and *logic* and by equating the mystical with the emotional, Crane arrived at his final conception of the logic of poetry.[7]

His essay "Modern Poetry," which gives the fullest expression of that conception, contains probably more philosophic and aesthetic confusions per sentence than any similar statement by any major poet. They are so serious and so numerous that to analyze them all would require a long essay in itself, and to do so would be to indulge in an exercise of dubious worth. But a knowledge of the chief ideas is a necessary preliminary to an analysis of the failure of *The Bridge* as myth. What then were Crane's final ideas of the nature of poetry?

First in the order which Crane gave them is the idea that the poet must be, as Emerson thought, a seer, a prophet, and a representative man. It is difficult to paraphrase Crane's words; I shall let him speak for himself:

> The poet's concern must be, as always, self-discipline toward a formal integration of experience. For poetry is an architectural art, based not on Evolution or the idea of progress, but on the articulation of the contemporary human consciousness *sub specie aeternitatis,* and inclusive of all re-

[7] Although I have thus, writing from the point of view of a Christian realist and rationalist, characterized Crane's doctrine as a confusion, what seems to me essential is not that all should agree to such a characterization, but that we should clearly recognize what Crane was doing in combining the Richards and the Ouspensky doctrines. A mystical doctrine of knowledge is intellectually respectable, though in my view inadequate unless corrected by respect for reason, and always open to dangerous abuses; the sort of behaviorist doctrine of knowledge widely held in the twenties and enunciated by Mr. Richards in his early works is not intellectually respectable; and the two are incompatible. On the other hand, in Crane's favor it may be said that many of our best literary critics today seem to share the belief of W. M. Urban (*Language and Reality*) that metaphor is the fundamental intuitive avenue to reality.

adjustments incident to science and other shifting factors related to that consciousness.

The rest of the paragraph is concerned with a different matter entirely and need not concern us (though one notes that Crane's lack of ability to think clearly and logically is apparent even in the structure of his prose paragraphs). What does this statement of the poet's "concern" mean?

It means first, perhaps, that Crane was conceiving of poetry not in imagist but in essentially philosophical or mythical terms. A "formal integration" of experience is what Dante achieved for his time and Crane attempted for his. Poetry so conceived might be called "architectural" in the sense that architecture is a logical and formal art which stands in an expressive relation to its time. The statement "means" that Crane wanted to become a synthesizer and a prophet like Whitman.

This aspect of the meaning of the passage is borne out by much of the rest of the essay. Poetry, Crane tells us, must "absorb" the machine, and the poet must surrender himself to the sensations of urban life. "The function of poetry in a machine age is identical to its function in any other age; and its capacities for presenting the most complete synthesis of human values remain essentially immune from any of the so-called inroads of science." Science is not really unfriendly to poetry; the poet must know science and use it. The future of American poetry is complicated because

Involved in it are the host of considerations relative to the comparative influences of science, machinery, and other factors. . . .

163

Whitman is the model for contemporary American poets because

> He, better than any other, was able to co-ordinate these forces in America which seem most intractable, fusing them into a universal vision which takes on additional significance as time goes on.

But one can become convinced that this is the meaning of the initial statement of the poet's concern only if he disregards the rest of the essay. For the prophetic-logical-architectural meanings, the attraction to the Emerson-Whitman conception of poetry, this "meaning" is balanced by the ideas Crane had taken from Mr. Eliot and Mr. Richards. One may begin with the first passage I quoted above and see that the contradiction between a desire to "synthesize" and a fear of the didactic is "resolved" by reliance on Ouspensky. The poet will "integrate" experience and take account of "shifting factors" like science, but what he will articulate will nevertheless be "consciousness," not knowledge or experience after all, and he will articulate it *sub specie aeternitatis.* (Ouspensky recommended achieving "cosmic consciousness.") So, too, in the later passages, it is said to be "questionable at best" that the modern poet can write philosophical or theological verse. "Science, the uncanonized deity of the times, seems to have automatically [*sic*] displaced the hierarchies of both Academy and Church." But the poet need fear no conflict with science, for "the 'truth' which science pursues is radically different from the metaphorical, extra-logical 'truth' of the poet." (Mr. Richards enters again, with a half-truth.) If one wonders at this point how the "extra-logical" truth of poetry can express science and synthesize science and religion, Crane has what he thought was a plausible answer ready: "Poetic prophecy in the case of the seer has nothing to do with factual prediction or with futurity."

This is just as clear as the notion that poetry is at once architectural and mystical. If neither idea is clear, the reason is not far to seek: "Modern Poetry" records Crane's desire to be a prophetic poet without being untrue to the poetic theory which was the last word in criticism in the twenties, the theory that, since only science conveys valid knowledge, poetry must limit itself to the organizing of the emotions and "attitudes" (Mr. Richards), that a poet must *feel,* not think (Mr. Eliot), that in short "A poem should not mean but be." So it is that all of Crane's longer poems, beginning with "The Marriage of Faustus and Helen," have philosophic intentions but often hide their intentions behind an obscurity sometimes consciously contrived.[8] And this conflict between Crane's ambition and his aesthetic theory accounts for more than it has been common to recognize. Crane's fundamental aim in his later poetry was incompatible with any theory which emphasizes emotion at the expense of sense. True, the logic of ordinary discourse is not the only kind of "logic," though it seems pointless to confuse the meaning of a useful word by applying it to what I should call non-logical forms of symbolism. The metaphorical symbolism of poetry conveys valid intuitive knowledge. But "the logic of ecstasy" is, if anything, mystical; and mystics do not "synthesize" bodies of knowledge or, as mystics at least, articulate myths representative of their age.[9]

[8] See the manuscript changes noted by Weber in *Hart Crane.*
[9] The "archetypal image" may arise from the unconscious, as Dr.

Though myths and philosophies are often based on their insights, both philosophy and myth are vitally concerned with knowledge available to the senses and organized in terms of reason. It is a question whether mystics ever communicate their mystic knowledge. If, as I think, they can evoke it if not precisely communicate it, then it seems likely that they can best do so through the metaphorical language of poetry. But even when they are gifted as poets, what they evoke is insights, not systems or syntheses or myths. And when they attempt to make their insights fully meaningful by placing them in a frame of reference, they adopt—or occasionally invent—a philosophical or theological or mythical system, usually taking over the one appropriate to their time, whether that be the Christianity of Meister Eckhart or the romantic naturalism of Emerson. Ouspensky's "logic of ecstasy," in short, did not eliminate, but only hid, the contradictions between Crane's theory of poetry and his aims as a poet. Unresolved, those contradictions run straight through all his major work, deepening the confusions that grew from another source.

3. Lead Me Past Logic

"God knows," Crane wrote to Waldo Frank in 1928, "some kind of substantial synthesis of opinion is needed before I can feel confident in writing about anything but my shoestrings. . . . These Godless days!" Such a synthesis

Jung believes, but the elaboration of the implications of the image into a poetic myth seems to me to call for the intervention of the conscious, "logical" mind. Thus Dante's Beatrice may be read as an *anima image,* but *The Divine Comedy* has the structure of art and of logic, not of dream. See Dr. Jung's *Psychological Types* (London, 1923) and *Psychology and Religion* (New Haven, 1938).

as Crane wanted is the work of myth and metaphysic. Lacking either, Crane tried to construct a myth of his own out of the materials at hand—science, Whitman, Whitehead, Spengler, and Ouspensky. (Not Eliot, for Crane misunderstood his position, thought of it only as pessimistic, cynical.) Considering the nature of his intellectual environment, the character of his chief sources of ideas, and his own unstable, undisciplined, and far from logical temperament, it is not surprising that the myth that resulted from the effort fell to pieces before it was finished.

That Crane recognized the cultural situation for what it was, that he felt the need of myth if poetry about anything more complicated than a simple sensate object were to be possible, is indicative of a fundamental perceptiveness which is not to be gainsaid by noting his lack of clear, logical thinking. Crane had the insights that come to genius. He was no philosopher, but a philosophy is valid only so far as the insights on which it is based are valid. Man cannot escape by logic, ecstatic or sober, from the relativity imposed finally by his occupation of a point in space and time. (Which does not absolve us from the obligation to make our ideas as clear and valid as may be.)

Lacking as he did a thorough education, Crane was thrown back exclusively upon the resources of his own time in his search for a system of meaning that would satisfy his intuitions and do justice to his knowledge. His knowledge was slight, but a part of it was the knowledge that the spirit of his age, of the twenties, was a spirit of positivism, materialism, naturalism. Nature had been divested of value, and man was rapidly being reduced to nature with no remainder. Philosophy, like history, was the bunk, and religion was delusion. In an age which more and more people are coming to feel was the nadir of Western philosophical and religious development, an era in which many felt with Conrad Aiken that the only finally certain sounds were those that composed "the melody of chaos," Crane searched for clues to the meaning of the sounds which he heard and which he tentatively identified as the treading of the heel of Elohim. Crane's was the search of a religious mystic for a system of belief.

The fact that his mother was a Christian Scientist, and that he was strongly attached to his mother, did not help. The only form of Christianity with which Crane had any intimate acquaintance seemed to him all too obviously a half-truth, a valuable comfort perhaps to ailing people like his mother but not to be taken seriously as a theology. Crane turned to philosophy for his beliefs. Whitehead, whose *Science and the Modern World* Crane read soon after it was published, helped to free him from dependence on the superstitions of materialistic naturalism. The great prestige which the book soon gained and kept certainly helped Crane to feel a part of a philosophical community.[10] Its philosophy of organic naturalism probably seemed to Crane, so far as he understood it, to confirm Whitman. Certainly Whitehead's chapter on religion, with its argument that science and religion do not really conflict and its authoritative recognition of the validity of mysticism, expressed ideas of the very sort for which Crane wanted proof.

But Whitehead was too abstruse a philosopher for his system to lend itself to myth-making. (Though his influ-

[10] For a view of the prestige which *Science and the Modern World* had among writers and thinkers of the twenties and thirties, see Malcolm Cowley and Bernard Smith (eds.), *Books That Changed Our Minds* (New York, 1939).

ence has been great, even his followers still differ over what he meant.) More suited to Crane's purpose was a book less respectable in philosophical circles, Ouspensky's *Tertium Organum*. A mixture of occultism, non-Euclidean geometries, Einsteinian physics, and traditional mysticism, it was the call of a mystical Russian mathematician for modern man to rise above materialism to the level of cosmic consciousness where the logic of ecstasy would make man godlike in perfect knowledge. It was Crane's chief source of information about the new world pictured by Einsteinian physics, and its facile use of non-Euclidean geometries to discredit traditional logic provided Crane with a rationale for his temperamental and environmental necessities. Its "mathematics of the infinite" included such axioms as "A magnitude cannot be equal to itself," and "ALL DIFFERENT magnitudes are equal among themselves," axioms very convenient to a mystic without a myth. Ouspensky's influence was almost certainly the greatest single one to which Crane was subject in the realm of ideas; it is to be seen both in the total intention of *The Bridge* and in discrete passages. A man must find his intellectual nourishment where he can, and it is probably pointless to regret that Crane found it in Ouspensky. No doubt the spiritualism of the *Tertium Organum,* which seems to me to have many affinities with the Christian Science which Crane had rejected, was the most adequate religion which, under the circumstances, Crane was capable of absorbing and profiting by.

Still, it was not enough, even for him. It is true, obviously, that no explanation of his increasingly rapid alternations between faith and despair on the basis solely of an inadequate belief is satisfactory. But neither is a purely psychological explanation. The enemies of Crane who see him only as an extreme neurotic whose ideas may be explained away by his compulsions err as much in one direction as Mr. Winters in another. (Man is both a creature and a spirit.) And so, impelled by a multitude of causes, some of which were connected with the tenuousness of his faith, Crane moved back and forth between the cynicism and despair of "the modern temper" and an exaltation of religious belief which came increasingly to require external stimulus for its arrival. That Crane's religious beliefs came to require an alcoholic base no more impugns the beliefs themselves than does the fact that his most terrible doubts were suffered on the mornings after. Spengler—whose *Decline of the West* Crane knew early and thoroughly, rejected often, and returned to always in his moments of despair—was simply the expression for Crane of the negation of the myth for which he was groping.[11] For Crane, Spengler summed up the essentials of modern pessimistic naturalism: he was one of the two poles between which Crane oscillated. But if it had not been Spengler's work, it would have been some other. Spengler was the label Crane attached to his doubts.

His doubts were frequent, and terrible. How could they have been other? Crane was no Frost, sturdy, skeptical, common-sensical, able to rest in the sufficiency of the moment. His faith was insecure and he knew it, inadequate and he probably did not know it.

The spiritual disintegration of our period becomes more

[11] "At times it seems demonstrable that Spengler is quite right," Crane wrote once; and again, "Yes, I read the whole of Spengler's book. It is stupendous . . . ." (Weber, *Hart Crane,* 282, 291.) But a Spenglerian outlook, as Crane well knew, was inconsistent with the purpose of *The Bridge.*

painful to me every day, so much so that I now find myself baulked by doubt at the validity of practically every metaphor that I coin.[12]

All that he could fall back on was the desperate hope that Ouspensky was right, that ordinary logic was no criterion of truth, that the intuitions of his moments of ecstasy were to be depended upon. "Lead me past logic," he cried, in a line once intended for use in "Cape Hatteras,"[13] past logic to a faith which neither Whitehead nor Ouspensky, Whitman nor his mother could give him, and which he desperately desired.

4. *The Broken Parabola*

In the Proem, "To Brooklyn Bridge," which is surely one of the most magnificent of modern poems, a triumph of applied science is celebrated as a symbol of achievement both material and spiritual. Here is concrete and beautiful evidence of the skills of the engineers, but here also is a suggestion of a mythic curve. The shape of the bridge is that of a promise; incomplete, demanding completion along lines already laid down, it unites vitality and form in a highly evocative symbol. To a poet, if not to a geometer, it suggests the perfect circle of the mystics, but it challenges the symbolizing activity in man to complete the circle; it suggests the ultimate symbol of physical science, the Einsteinian cosmos of finite but unbounded space; it points ahead to the passage in "Cape Hatteras" beginning

12 Weber, *Hart Crane*, 299.
13 *Ibid.*, 367.

But that star-glistered salver of infinity,
The circle, blind crucible of endless space,
Is sluiced by motion—subjugated never.

Yet at the same time it never ceases to be the parabolic
sweep of Brooklyn Bridge, very real, very concrete, con-
necting Brooklyn and Manhattan as well as the spheres.
Since it is not a part of my purpose to attempt complete critical assessments of any of the poems I discuss in
this study, I shall not comment on the many magnificent
lines in the poem or on its perfectly mastered structure;
but because I have already indicated my opinion that
The Bridge fails as myth, I should like to say now that if
Crane had written nothing else but the Proem his name
would be an important one in modern poetry.

But before turning to the rest of *The Bridge* I should
like to note two features of this poem that are very relevant to the purposes of this study. First, the poem indicates—symbolically, I should say it achieves—that union
of the sensible and the conceptual, the world of experience and the world of physical theory, which the Einstein
of Mr. McLeish's poem of that name failed to achieve.
With the mystic's solvent vision Crane sees the traffic
lights against the "unfractioned idiom" of the now greatly expanded parabola as "immaculate sigh of stars." In
flashes of insight gained in the composition of his poetry
—not, apparently, in his life outside his poetry—Crane
did achieve something of the vision for which he longed.
But insights demand interpretation, and interpretation
requires a suitable frame of reference, a philosophy or a
myth; which takes us back to Crane's failure, without,
however, lessening the achievement.

Second, the bridge of the Proem moves as a symbol

from concrete to abstract, from physical to spiritual, from limited to infinite suggestiveness, by a motion so gradual that it is impossible to detect, yet equally impossible to deny. Crane's power as a lyric poet is nowhere better indicated than in this gradual transmutation of the bridge symbol. More subtle than the shifts in the symbolism of the annunciation in the lyric in "The Dry Salvages," this poetic sleight of hand takes us, as it took Crane, close to the comprehension which he desired and we desire. We are ready, profoundly yet unconsciously prepared, at the end, for

> *O Sleepless as the river under thee,*
> *Vaulting the sea, the prairies' dreaming sod,*
> *Unto us lowliest sometime sweep, descend*
> *And of the curveship lend a myth to God.*

So the Proem has prepared us for a work which will celebrate man's conquest of space—physically, as in the bridge, intellectually, as in the scientific knowledge that made the bridge possible and that reveals that the curve of the bridge is a segment of the curve of cosmic space, and finally, as in religious myth. Einsteinian science has become something more than arcane formulae; it has taken on the character of revelation, revealing the relationship of the curve of the bridge and the curve of the cosmos and the light of the traffic signals and of the stars. And of this complex revelation Crane has forged a unity, so that all things, bridge, knowledge that made it possible, even the darkness in which the shadow of the bridge attains its only clarity, point to one end: the symbol of man's completion of the curve, the final word in the poem, God.

173

Since *The Bridge* has been elaborately analyzed by others, and especially since Mr. Weber's long and helpful comment and paraphrase is now available, I shall touch only the points most relevant to this study in the remainder of my remarks. "Ave Maria," which follows the Proem, strengthens the idea already lightly suggested in the Proem that science is behind and faith before discovery; that, in terms of the poem, Columbus' discovery rested on the newly improved science of navigation but was stimulated and guided by faith. So science, operating as an aspect of man's reading of the General Revelation, explores nature and so reveals God. Like Newton and the deists, Crane in this section declares (what he had already hinted in the Proem) his faith that science and intuition work together for religious ends:

> *Of all that amplitude that time explores,*
> *A needle in the sight, suspended north,—*
> *Yielding by inference and discard, faith*
> *And true appointment from the hidden shoal:*
> *This disposition that thy night relates*
> *From Moon to Saturn in one sapphire wheel:*
> *The orbic wake of thy once swirling feet,*
> *Elohim, still I hear thy sounding heel!*

Inference and faith descry the Reality: here, in this great conclusion to an uneven section, in the final stanza, ending with traditional Christian and mystic overtones in

> *Te Deum laudamus*
>
> *O Thou Hand of Fire*

as much as in the stanza I quoted above, Crane achieves a momentary companionship with the great expositors of the traditional faith.

"Harbor Dawn" and "Van Winkle" and the opening section of "The River" represent, among other things such as the search for a distinctly American basis for the myth, the "absorbing" of the sensations of contemporary urban life which Crane thought necessary to the poet as representative man. Here we are back again with applied science and sensate experience of physical facts, where we began at the opening of the Proem. The implication is that even urban life, with its noise, its vulgarity, its splintering of the unified consciousness approached at the end of the Proem and again in the conclusion of "Ave Maria," is no real barrier to the mystic discovery. This at least seems to be the chief intended meaning of the poems. Actually, Crane's attitude toward contemporary urban America was a dual one of affirmation and distaste; he did not succeed in purifying his intention in these poems, so that affirmation is only partially achieved. But that it is the chief intention is clear from the fact that the satire of such lines as those that precede and follow "SCIENCE —COMMERCE and the HOLYGHOST" in "The River" strikes us as discordant. It is out of place because it denies what is intended to be affirmed: Whitman's vision that science applied, like science pure, contains a promise of "wisdom, power, and grace."

In "The Dance," Maquokeeta seems to represent, as Mr. Weber suggests, the conquest of space, physical, scientific, and mystical as in the Proem. The brave is perhaps God. But it is impossible for me to read this section with an assurance of understanding. Following a section, "The River," the last half of which seems to me one of the finest things in all modern poetry, this section strikes me as very obscure. Perhaps it is significant that in it a mystic frenzy and a corrosive doubt are side by side. In its praise of the warrior's return to the soil, in the hymn to death, it takes the perennial mystic way: first, magnification of the spiritual as distinct from the natural self, then obliteration of all identity, spiritual as well as natural, in union with the timeless and perfect All. This is the way of Eastern mysticism—raising oneself above the flux, then extinguishing oneself in the Not-Being; this was also Emerson's way, for self-reliance turned out in the end to lead to automatism, the magnified individual to be but a fragment of the perfect and perfectly necessary sum total of things, the Oversoul. This is Crane's way, and he asserts it, as I have said, frenziedly, as Whitman had asserted it calmly in "When Lilacs" and elsewhere. But perhaps his frenzy is a factor of his doubt; for there is a crucial uncertainty in the stanza which immediately precedes the climactic identification of Crane with the warrior:

> Spark, tooth! Medicine-man, relent, restore—
> Lie to us,—dance us back the tribal morn!

The tribal morn will not return, and Crane knew it. His frenzy was worked up in self-defense, defense of his Ouspenskian self against his Spenglerian self.

Of "Indiana" there is no need here to make any analysis. I have commented elsewhere on the connection between its sentimentality and Crane's recurrent nihilism (Crane wrote the section near the end of his work on *The Bridge,* when faith in his myth was almost completely gone); and it is clear, too, that Crane's personality was such that it was difficult or impossible for him to realize other people clearly and objectively, with sympathy but without sentimentality. The section is the poorest in *The*

Bridge; indeed, it is difficult to imagine that the poet who wrote it also wrote the Proem.

"Cutty Sark" seems to me not one of the greatest sections because of its too great reliance on the deliberate incoherence of the stream-of-consciousness method, but it is hauntingly beautiful in parts and will be remembered as one of the finest impressionistic poems of our time. There seems to me to be nothing in it which demands special comment from the point of view of this study.

"Cape Hatteras" is, as I have said, the most explicit internal clue to the meaning of the poem. Flawed and terribly uneven, it rises to heights almost as great as those of the finest sections of *The Bridge* and sinks to depths nearly as low as those of "Indiana." Preceded by a quotation from Whitman, it opens with what seems to me a remarkably vivid and suggestive evocation of the world, first as geology, then as modern physics reveals it. But my "first, then" falsifies the situation: the vision is total, geological-physical, the physical world of all modern knowledge, in which geological evidence of the rising and falling of the land masses and Einsteinian evidence of the nature of the cosmos are blended:

> *Imponderable the dinosaur*
> > *sinks slow,*
> > > *the mammoth saurian*
> > > *ghoul, the eastern*
> > > > *Cape . . . .*
>
> *While rises in the west the coastwise range,*
> > *slowly the hushed land—*
>
> *Combustion at the astral core—the dorsal change*
> *Of energy—convulsive shift of sand . . . .*

The first verse-paragraph closes by returning to the spirit of Whitman: "Or to read you, Walt,—knowing us in thrall." The suggestion here is that Whitman's verse contains all this evocation of space and time, of the mystery of the physical cosmos and the imaginative implications of science—as indeed it does. The second paragraph proceeds through references to the soil, both geologically and mythically considered, to time, contained in "those folded eons"—a nice example of a highly condensed figure—through the sounds of radio static ("The captured fume of space foams in our ears") to an attitude of half-frustrated, half-hopeful search, as one peering through a periscope or caught in a labyrinth searches.

The next section, which brings to a climax these opening three paragraphs, suggests what we see as we peer through the periscope and glimpse the reality which lies beyond our direct vision.

> But that star-glistered salver of infinity,
> The circle, blind crucible of endless space,
> Is sluiced by motion,—subjugated never.

These and the lines that follow can only be understood in Einsteinian terms; and they are all understandable. Motion, "subjugated never," is basic in a world from which the concept of absolute rest has been eliminated; Einsteinian cosmology conceives space as circular and proves that the curve of the bridge is paralleled in the curve of light. The lines beginning "Adam and Adam's answer" present the same problem of solipsism that Mr. MacLeish treated in "Einstein." The eagle which, in the next several lines, is said to "dominate our days" is space. The next sentence, beginning "Space, instantaneous, Flickers a moment, consumes us in its smile," continues

the subject of the effect on modern sensibility of the newly achieved freedom, both physical and imaginative, in
space. But the freeing of the body from some of its spatial
limitations through the airplane and other devices and of
the senses through the radio and so on, the drastic re-
vision, in short, of man's physical relation to space, and
the revolutionary shift in his concept of space through
the coming of Einsteinian physics—these have a double-
edged significance; and it is on this note that the paragraph closes:

> *Dream cancels dream in this new realm of fact*
> *From which we wake into the dream of act:*
> *Seeing himself an atom in a shroud—*
> *Man hears himself an engine in a cloud!*

The first two of these closing lines I take to refer to
the disharmony between the Einsteinian description of
reality and the reality which man perceives through sense
and realizes in action; and to the abstrusely mathematical
character of the new knowledge, the apparent lack of
solidity of the world which it describes being equaled
only by the dreamlike quality which in certain peculiar
moments ordinary experience sometimes has; and finally
to the age-old problem of the ultimate uncertainty of
all man's knowledge, an uncertainty which Hume and
Berkeley demonstrated for all time. The last two lines,
in addition to foreshadowing the later introduction of
the airplane as a symbol of spatial conquest, seem to me
to contrast the world of classical physics—man an "atom"
in a world of dead matter—with that of modern physics,
in which dead matter has been dissolved and the crucial
significance of the knowing mind has been emphasized,

as it has been in operational philosophies of science like that of Mr. Bridgman and in the Uncertainty Principle of quantum physics as well as in the over-all and basic Theory of Relativity of Einstein, in which the perspective of the observer has everything to do with what is observed. But the contrast between the two worlds is not one that suggests simple advance: not outmoded physics, which placed man in a shroud, happily supplanted by the new physics; for it is not entirely to man's liking to be in a cloud either. Again, dream cancels dream, and we search for the final reality in vain so long as we stay within the area of natural knowledge.

Finally, the last two lines also suggest another difference between the old physics and the new, or, rather, between the two worlds which they present to the mind. The old or classical physics was a sort of codification and refinement of common sense and sense experience, a refinement which ultimately cleared away in the refining process nearly all recognizable elements of that experience and left it merely a curious anomoly in a meaningless world. (As Whitehead has put it, "Dead nature can give no reasons . . . . All ultimate reasons are in terms of aim at value.")[14] The new physics begins by discarding sense and relying on "pointer readings," which yield a highly indirect knowledge of the objects under study, on the use of conceptual reason in general, and, particularly, on mathematics. One "sees" the matter of the old physics, if not atoms, then chunks of atoms, dust, ashes, stones, flesh; one must accept the report of the physicist, whose procedures for obtaining his conclusions one cannot follow, if one is to know Eddington's table as electrons and

[14] *Nature and Life* (Chicago, 1934), 8.

protons and (mostly) empty space. The new knowledge is "extrasensate"; one only "hears" about the world which it declares to be the real one.

All this—and much more—is in these lines. The paragraph is as clear as anything in Crane's work, though it is difficult to make an explication of it clear, so dense are the lines, as clear as it could well be and preserve its immense suggestiveness; and it is a more compact and informed evocation of the physical world as modern man knows it than any other passage of poetry that I know of. It, and other passages like it, give Crane a unique place in modern American poetry. For Crane surpassed Mr. MacLeish in the one area of sensibility in which MacLeish achieved something really distinctive in his poetry. If in my comments I have made the passage in question seem like a piece of poetic pedantry or an effort, like Erasmus Darwin's, to rhyme scientific knowledge, the fault lies in the clumsiness of the comment, not in the verse. The knowledge that underlies the lines is neither deep nor wide: it is probable that Crane got it all from Ouspensky; but it is precisely the kind of knowledge that he needed to do the kind of job he was trying to do in *The Bridge*. It does, in a very real sense, articulate an aspect, and a very important aspect, of contemporary consciousness. Only to those —and they are many, even among the most skilled readers of modern poetry—who are still living in the Newtonian world of their high-school physics course will the passage seem pointless or unnecessarily obscure. Although it is common to condemn "Cape Hatteras" *in toto* as one of the weakest sections of *The Bridge*, this opening passage and certain other shorter ones in the poem are unequaled in contemporary verse.

The next paragraph turns to Whitman again: he sensed infinity as he walked the beach at Paumanak, he wandered in the labyrinth but caught the gleam of light beyond, his eyes were "Sea eyes and tidal, undenying, bright with myth!" It was in this paragraph that Crane originally called upon Whitman to lead him past logic. The essence of the service which Whitman is called upon to perform is still clear without the line; but the way in which he can perform it is not at all clear, either here or elsewhere in the whole poem. (When we approach the center of the myth, we find everywhere silence, which may be the silence of the mystic who finds it impossible to communicate his vision, but also suggests the silence enforced by a failure of ideas.)

The verse that follows confesses the difficulty of re-capturing the sense of infinity and the vision that Whitman had; for meanwhile "The nasal whine of power whips a new universe" (the dynamo symbol of Henry Adams and the electrical nature of matter declared by the new physics), and

> Stars prick the eyes with sharp ammoniac proverbs,
> New virtues, new inklings in the velvet hummed
> Of dynamos, where hearing's leash is strummed . . .
> Power's script,—wound, bobbin-bound, refined—
> Is stropped to the slap of belts on booming spools,
>   spurred
> Into the bulging bouillion, harnessed jelly of
>   the stars.
> Towards what?

Whitman thought he knew what it was all going towards; Crane hoped he might discover, sometimes persuading himself that he knew. (But it seems to me unlikely that

a satisfactory myth can ever be based on hope, moments
of mystical awareness, and self-deception.)

The three paragraphs that follow are intended to be,
and actually begin by being, two-leveled. They equate
the imaginative grasp of space which has just been presented with the physical conquest of space symbolized
by the airplane. The imaginative achievement comes first,
in the opening lines:

> *Stars scribble on our eyes the frosty sagas,*
> *The gleaming cantos of unvanquished space ....*

Then the lines turn to the "sinewy silver biplane," the
sense of space is lost in a stream of thin rhetoric celebrating the Wright brothers and the possibility that we shall
some day fly to Mars, and the whole passage ends by seeming only silly. The failure here, unlike the larger failure
of *The Bridge,* is one of technique (the verse does not
maintain the promised two levels of meaning), and of
taste (the Wright brothers and the Sunday-supplement
news about Mars hardly inspire us with a sense of the
arcane magnificence of space). Yet the intention of the
section is, like that of "Cape Hatteras" as a whole, to
grasp the imaginative identity of the worlds revealed by
applied science, pure science, and intuition; or action, understanding, and reason; or the physical, the rational,
and the spiritual; and thus to "conjugate infinity's dim
marge."

The final part of the poem, beginning after the break
indicated by Crane, seems to me to maintain a consistently higher level than the parts preceding, though no
lines in it equal those first three paragraphs on which
I have commented at length. Whitman is called upon

again, the geological vision is reinvoked in the line which includes "tides awash the pedestal of Everest," wars, geography, and man's perversity are taken into account, and the final magnificent paean is begun with "Cowslip and shad-blow, flaked with tethered foam." This leads into the climactic statement of why Whitman is the guiding spirit of the poem:

> *O, something green,*
> *Beyond all sesames of science was thy choice*
> *Wherewith to bind us throbbing with one voice . . . .*

Now finally, at the end of the section, the verse achieves the promised (and required) two-leveled intensity, forging the airplane into the symbol it was meant to be all along, binding in one figure all the spatial revolutions of modern life and thought and the mystical significance of the new achievements and knowledge:

> *And now, as launched in abysmal cupolas of space,*
> *Toward endless terminals, Easters of speeding light—*
> *Vast engines outward veering with seraphic grace*
> *On clarion cylinders pass out of sight*
> *To course that span of consciousness thou'st named*
> *The Open Road—thy vision is reclaimed!*
> *What heritage thou'st signalled to our hands!*

So the section ends with Crane dedicating himself and his poem to Whitman's kind of transcendentalism, a mysticism "inclusive" of science and the machine, yet also both fundamentally and ultimately intuitive:

> *My hand*
> *in yours,*
> *Walt Whitman—*
>
> *so—*

The next section, "Three Songs," has, as it has often been remarked, no clear function in the development of the theme of *The Bridge*. "Quaker Hill," too, seems to me to make little contribution to the theme of the poem of which it is formally a part, though as an excursion into personal history it may be said to prepare the way for the next section, "The Tunnel." (But since "Three Songs" has already provided the contrast needed to emphasize the heights attained at the end of "Cape Hatteras" and to maintain the rhythm of alternating fact and value that runs throughout the poem, we do not need the further deflation of "Quaker Hill.")

"The Tunnel" is one of the finest sections in the whole poem. Now the elevators have dropped us from our day and we grope through the labyrinth. Preceding the ecstatic affirmation of the final section, "The Tunnel" maintains that rhythm of light and dark, skepticism and faith, depression and exaltation, of which I have just spoken and which is an essential part of the structure of the poem. It is perhaps unnecessary to say that the poem's failure is not a result of this rhythmic ambiguity, but of Crane's failure to maintain the rhythm and the related failure to provide any logical progression of theme like the progression in the Proem and the artistically flawed but logically tenable progression in "Cape Hatteras." The rhythm is not maintained, the theme does not progress: here, for example, in "The Tunnel," the skepticism is too final even for a plan which calls for alternations of mood. It reveals the preceding affirmations as rather wished for than achieved vision. Although it cannot cancel the moments of mystic intuition, it can destroy their value for the myth:

185

Performances, assortments, résumés—
. . . You shall search them all.
Some day you'll learn each famous sight
And watch the curtain lift in hell's despite.

One had thought he felt the curtain lifting somewhat, but it has dropped again if so, and we are now not as far along toward the achievement of the mythic faith as we were at the end of the Proem. The progression of the poem is superficial—a matter of the structural rhythm I have spoken of—and fragmentary—a matter of progression within the discrete parts.

Out of all the many great lines and passages in the section, I want to comment on just two. The first, beginning "Daemon, demurring and eventful yawn," expresses in accents of despair the very "cosmic consciousness" recommended by Ouspensky and to an extent achieved earlier in the poem. Evidently cosmic consciousness is not enough. There are practical problems which it does not meet and hastening dooms which it does not prevent:

O cruelly to innoculate the brinking dawn
With antennae toward worlds that glow and sink;—
To spoon us out more liquid than the dim
Locution of the eldest star, and pack
The conscience navelled in the plunging wind,
Umbilical to call—and straightway die!

Mystic transcendentalism and cosmic consciousness are not enough when we cannot repress the thought that we shall straightway die. They emphasize how much we have been given, only to re-emphasize how utterly it is all destroyed. Sharpening the outlines of the paradox, they turn it into a cruel joke. And it does not help, either, to assert, as in "The Dance," that we shall be returning to what produced us: though the conscience may be "na-velled in the plunging wind," it is not, after all, like the wind, a merely physical force. The lines I have quoted from "The Tunnel" have great beauty and power, but they negate rather than affirm the validity of the myth which the poem as a whole is attempting to express. And their negation is such that no succeeding affirmation can entirely erase their effect, for they show the inadequacy of the myth as such rather than the force of opposing facts. Ouspensky was not a sufficient answer to Spengler.

The next paragraph maintains the splendor of lan-guage and continues the mood of depression, but it turns midway to the hope, to the almost forgotten promise. Yet, significantly, the attempted reaffirmation is made in terms not of cosmic consciousness but of Christian faith. Al-though that faith is equated with mysticism in general, "Lazarus" and the "Word" dominate the passage sym-bolically, as, after the next paragraph, the "Hand of Fire" dominates the conclusion and turns the tunnel into Pur-gatory. But this Christian symbolism, which here has en-tered without preparation, is not developed in the next and concluding section, "Atlantis," except by the several references to the bridge as a bridge to Love. So one can only conclude that, with his faith in the original outlines of his myth weakening, Crane was groping for other affir-mations to buttress his crumbling structure. (True, the dear love of comrades is a chief theme in Whitman, but Crane's invocation of the master had been in terms only of his "vision.") That the new "affirmations" for which the poem at this point seems to be searching might, like Christianity, be quite different from the one which he had promised in the Proem and constructed fragments of elsewhere did not, in Crane's extremity, much matter. Any hope, however un-Whitmanic, was welcome:

And yet, like Lazarus, to feel the slope,
The sod and billow breaking,—lifting ground,
—A sound of waters bending astride the sky
Unceasing with some Word that will not die . . . !

Like "Cape Hatteras" with its unfortunate passage celebrating the airplane, "Atlantis" is weakened by the stanzas which appear to sing the praises of tall buildings. The obscurity of this passage is significant: it is an attempt once again to express the faith that had been destroyed by the mood of "Quaker Hill" and "The Tunnel." (Even though Crane did not write the sections of *The Bridge* in the order in which they now appear, biographical analysis, as Mr. Weber has shown, supports the thesis that Crane lost faith in his myth before he had finished composing the poem.) Although the lines on tall buildings or whatever they are do convey a sense of soaring, of lift and aspiration, we are tempted by them to ask in Crane's own words, "Towards what?" But this "Psalm of Cathay" becomes clearer about halfway through and, beginning with "O thou steeled Cognizance whose leap commits," seems to me more nearly worthy of the great poem of which it is the conclusion. The "Cognizance" is, of course, Ouspensky's cosmic consciousness and mystic awareness in general; the "leap" is that which faith takes when it comes to the last of the proved or provable facts, a leap which goes beyond "time's realm."

But there is one obscurity in this stanza, an obscurity in a line verbally clear. The last line reads, "As love strikes clear direction for the helm." This could be the statement of a traditional Christian mystic. Should one, in view of the Lazarus and Word passage in the preceding section, take the hint and read this in Christian terms? Suggesting that one should is the line several stanzas above, "O Love, thy white, pervasive Paradigm"; but against such a reading there exists the whole body of the poem except for these passages. How can love be the paradigm of "cosmic consciousness"? True, Whitman's dear love of comrades had seemed to Whitman an axiom needing no philosophical or theological support. But if Crane expected his invocation of Whitman in "Cape Hatteras" to be sufficient basis for this sudden introduction of love as the paradigm at the end of his poem, he was greatly mistaken, and his poem suffers in consequence. I suggest that again, as in the preceding section, the introduction of a Christian term and concept is indicative of the breakdown of Crane's myth, or of his faith in his myth, indicative of a search for support from any source whatever. "Love" comes easily to modern lips (and as slow to modern as to ancient hearts); its use without preparation and definition is a form of sentimentality, just as its introduction as a new theme so late in the poem is an indication of structural breakdown. It seems to me that it is as sentimental and external here as it is in the ending of Thornton Wilder's novel, *The Bridge of San Luis Rey.*

At any rate, one thing is clear: "love" is not, even in this final, wavering, ambiguous section of the poem, Christian *caritas,* supported by a conception of man and his place and duty. The poem makes use of the suggestions attaching to a Christian term, but it is not a Christian poem. The next stanza starts, "Swift peal of secular light, intrinsic Myth," and we see that the light is still secular. Ouspensky's idea of a religion founded on the revelations of the new science is still the guiding concept. As the light is secular, so the myth is intrinsic, by which is meant, I take it, that it is natural, not supernatural, that it grows directly out of the facts of science. The "love" in the conclusion of *The Bridge* must be humanitarianism. It does not improve the poem as myth or as poetry.

So *The Bridge* ends in stanzas of uneven merit and ambiguous meaning. The myth has not been enunciated, it has been hinted at, glimpsed, promised. Strictly speaking, the poem itself has not been achieved.

5. *A Passage to India*

"For the Marriage of Faustus and Helen" had attempted to indicate a synthesis of knowledge and beauty, science and art. *The Bridge* attempted a task even more difficult, the creation of a myth that would unify all those "most intractable" forces in modern life, especially science and religion. It failed, but only when its accomplishment is compared with its aim. It failed, not in comparison with the poetry of its day, but in comparison with the great religious and mythic poems. It failed even as compared with "A Passage to India," for the discords it attempted to harmonize were greater and the harmonizing faith less secure. It is not, most people will agree, finally a poem at all except formally, but a group of poems, most of them on various aspects of a single theme. Some of them are among the finest poems of our time.

A considerable part of the value of these great poems lies just where Crane thought it lay, in their expression of the new, scientific, urban, spatial consciousness affected if not created by science pure and applied. The achieved content of *The Bridge*—and I am not talking now about content in abstraction but about content-as-expressed— the *achieved* content of *The Bridge* is an awareness of contemporary life and knowledge that approaches uniqueness in purity and intensity. Crane succeeded in one of his general aims, if he did not succeed in his specific aim in *The Bridge:* he expressed contemporary human consciousness, its heights and its depths, its insights and its blind spots.

And though his power was as a poet, not as a thinker, he was right in his thinking about many things. The poet needs a myth as much as ever; or rather, needs a suitable myth. (If he does not have a good one, he is very likely to have a bad one, like the myth of progress or the myth of blood and soil.) The two great conflicting forces of our day are, as Crane thought, knowledge and faith, fact and value. Probably, too, the poet today who would write significant philosophic poetry must, as Crane thought, "take account" of science and the machine, though not necessarily in so direct a way as Crane. The symbolism typical of science and the symbolism typical of poetry are, as Crane said, different, though, insofar as they both use words, they are alike in using words with regard for their denotations. (Science in some of its more exact forms drops words altogether.)

Crane was also wrong. It is not true that "poetic prophecy" has nothing to do with "factual prediction" or with "futurity." If it were true, it would mean either that the paraphrasable content of a poem is merely decoration, pseudo-statement, not to be taken seriously, in which case Crane's stated intentions for *The Bridge* may be dismissed; or that we are living in two perfectly discrete worlds, an aesthetic world and a scientific, practical, historical, and rational one, which is nonsense. No, one cannot be taken seriously as a poetic seer or prophet, as Crane hoped to be, if poetry is limited to the use of "emotive" language. Either poetry deals with, includes, *is* in some sense knowledge, or *The Bridge* should never have been attempted.

Fortunately it was attempted, and the great poems in it do not need the justification for their being which an adequate theory of poetry would provide. They justify themselves by their sensible magnificence. Crane had the true poet's gifts, the gift of insight and the gift of words. His *Bridge,* though as old as Whitman in conception, is as new as the latest revolution in physics in the character of its expressed vision. It is at once the great hymn to science of our time and a great mystical document evoking modern man's awareness of "this great wink of eternity." If its mystic curve finally descends in lower Manhattan instead of Cathay, it is still one of our richest and most exciting efforts to express a myth newly created to replace those of which the world has been "disabused," to lessen the "poverty of mind and unhappiness of life," and to satisfy in some degree the need which Crane expressed in "Voyages II":

> *Bind us in time, O Seasons clear, and awe.*
> *O minstrel galleons of Carib fire,*
> *Bequeath to us no earthly shore until*
> *Is answered in the vortex of our grave*
> *The seal's wide spindrift gaze toward paradise.*

192

VIII. Science and Poetry: Conclusions

> *All human knowledge is tainted with an "ideological" taint. It pretends to be more true than it is. It is finite knowledge, gained from a particular perspective; but it pretends to be final and ultimate knowledge.*
>
> —REINHOLD NIEBUHR *in* The Nature and Destiny of Man.

1. *Language, Myth, and Metaphysic*

Poets, it would seem, are not happy without myth or metaphysics or both. Myth is metaphysics in concrete terms, metaphysics translated into narrative and drama. Both myth and metaphysics represent the effort of the mind to reach beyond experience in order to give experience meaning, to generalize beyond the facts, to exceed the knowable that the knowable may be more truly known. One may say, with Mr. Ransom, that religious myth always involves the supernatural and that the assumptions of science, mathematical or physical, are supernatural in something like the same sense.[1] But perhaps *supernatural* does more to confuse than to clarify the issue. The logical positivists have recognized the fact here and would, up to a point, agree: for in outlawing the realms of moral, religious, and aesthetic thought, of all the humanistic disciplines, in fact, from the realm of

---

[1] *God Without Thunder* (New York, 1930), 65, 72 ff.

193

knowledge, and in insisting that even exact science is simply descriptive and nothing more, they are emphasizing, among other things, the fact that all man's knowledge rests on unproved and unprovable assumptions and that any truly meaningful generalizations from the "facts" of his knowledge always exceed the evidence. There is much more, of course, to logical positivism than this, but the younger adherents to the position—one can hardly call it a philosophy, since it classifies philosophy as nonsense—go much farther than simply, with the popular semanticists, calling value statements false or meaningless and the fact statements of the exact sciences true: this position of the early positivists has given way to a more thoroughgoing skepticism which finds any statement which exceeds a description of the relevant sensations or operations meaningless. So that the antirationalism of our time, starting as a defense of experimental science against metaphysics and religion, has ended by cutting the ground out from under science, too. Myth and metaphysics are not much worse off than science if the views of the extreme neo-nominalists are correct, for although according to these views science is important by virtue of its practical efficiency, it does not reveal reality; and if it does not reveal reality, it is not important for philosophy. (*Reality* itself is a meaningless noise, according to these views.)

But extreme logical positivism is actually, for all its bizarre consequences, no more interesting as philosophy than "semiotic" is as a theory of language. Both, I am willing to hazard, will some day be recognized as curious symptoms of a sick age. As Mr. Richards, apparently repenting of his early errors, has reminded us that *semantic* rhymes with *antic, frantic,* and *romantic,*[2] so I should like to point out that *semiotic* makes a nice feminine rhyme with *idiotic.* The division of the functions of language into the emotive and the referential, a division common to the logical positivists, to the early Mr. Richards (who in *The Meaning of Meaning, Science and Poetry,* and *The Principles of Literary Criticism* combined influences from the logical positivists with influences from the behaviorists to create the most typical and influential theory of language and literature of the time), and to most of the semanticists—this division, which leaves one no choice but to put poetry into the emotive classification, since it clearly is not referential in the way science is, is so patently inadequate that one would not dignify it with serious discussion at this date if it had not helped to shape the whole course of poetry and criticism from Mr. Eliot's early work on.

The poets have reacted in various ways to this emotive-referential theory of language; nearly all of the younger poets have been affected by it directly, and the older poets have responded to the general temper of which it is an extreme manifestation. Robinson's distrust of philosophy, of any generalized reasoning indeed, shows

[2] *Furioso,* Vol. I (Summer, 1941). I shall not attempt to substantiate my remarks on behavioristic semantics and semiotic: detailed discussion of the philosophy of language is beyond the scope of this work. But I refer interested readers to my earlier note on the critics of the original position of Mr. Richards on this matter; and as for Charles W. Morris's "semiotic," I refer the reader to Mr. Tate's "Literature as Knowledge" in *On the Limits of Poetry.* I think it is interesting that John Dewey, who is, I suppose, the greatest living exponent of scientific positivism, writing from within a frame of reference very different from my own, finds as little value in the semantics of Carnap and Morris as I do. See John Dewey and Arthur F. Bentley, *Knowing and the Known* (New York, 1949).

the influence of the modern low estimate of the power of reason and the word. Mr. Frost's skepticism, his conviction that the progress of philosophy is comparable to the motion of a caged bear as he rocks back and forth from cheek to cheek, is another indication of the same spirit at work. Some of the logical confusions in Mr. Eliot's critical theory speak eloquently of the same influence, though his poetry says something else again. Mr. Mac-Leish's "a poem should not mean but be" is another indication of the same spirit, and one that does not fit very neatly with his demand that poetry express a myth that man can believe in and take courage from. Hart Crane's logic of ecstasy is another. And many poets I have not treated exhibit traces of the same influence—Wallace Stevens, W. C. Williams, Allen Tate, nearly all of those who have followed the path first charted by Mr. Eliot.

But there is another point of view from which one may say that modern poetry has offered a corrective to inadequate positivistic theories of language. Forced by the trends of critical thinking to minimize the amount of "statement," of ordinary discursive symbolism, in their poetry, and not content, for the most part, to write "pure" —or "meaningless" or merely "emotive"—poetry, the poets have fallen back on what seems almost always to have been poetry's chief resource, a use of language which, though it is both referential and emotive, is not principally either, but intuitive or evocative. It is not accidental that modern critical study of the language of poetry has centered around the metaphor. For though by metaphor we point to objects and convey emotions, what we chiefly do is to convey knowledge by forging new symbols that are themselves patterns of meaning and that

196

impinge on, and sometimes rearrange, other patterns of meaning. Thus *Gestalt* psychology and modern poetic theory join hands to require the addition of a third function to the two of the positivists. And quite apart from theory, scientific or literary, there is the whole body of modern poetry itself, which cannot be understood or correctly evaluated in terms of a theory of language which makes all use of words either emotive or referential and nothing else.

Mr. Eliot's Quartets, for example, convey emotion and make some valid references to tangible refcients; but after these functions have been abstracted from them, there is something, indeed nearly everything, left over. What is left is normative knowledge conveyed by metaphor and structure and plain statement; in short, knowledge of values, variously conveyed. Poetry, modern or ancient, demands a more adequate theory of the uses of language than that in *The Meaning of Meaning* and in all the books that derive from that work. Considered as evidence of the possibilities inherent in language, poetry offers a corrective to the positivists. One must have reservations, I think, about all of the attempts to date to work out a more adequate systematic philosophy of language than that which issued in the referential-emotive classification; but I suspect that what will finally emerge will be a philosophy which will account for some of the facts pointed out by W. M. Urban in *Language and Reality* and which will add to the referential and the emotive uses of language at least one other, what T. C. Pollock calls the "evocative" use.[3]

[3] *The Nature of Literature: Its Relation to Science, Language, and Human Experience* (Princeton, N. J., 1942).

Meanwhile, whatever their theory of language, near-ly all the poets have rejected the materialist, positivist, behaviorist outlook, which is to say, the core of modernism. With few exceptions they have, as practicing poets, written as though values were real and objective, whatever their status in scientific philosophy. And as thinking men they have almost always longed for, accepted, or attempted to create a myth or a metaphysic which would explain the reality of value. The Purpose and the Law for which Robinson searched has been once and can be again defined by religion and philosophy, but Robinson was too much the child of the late nineteenth century to understand the nature and function of myth and reason. He searched the scientific books and could find no answer —naturally; he hoped that science would give the answer after it had reached "the jumping-off place," by which I suppose he meant after science had proceeded so far from common sense as to lead once again into what it started from, philosophy—as indeed the new physics has shown some signs of doing. But he could not wait for the answer, and science as science would not have supplied it anyway even if he had had more time at his disposal for waiting. His complex relation to myth—myth desired and myth denied—is one of the chief critical problems in his work.

Tough-minded Mr. Frost seems able to do without myth, but he pays a high price for his independence. He does not share Robinson's confusion of looking to science for answers which science cannot possibly give, for he thinks, with the rest of those who are adjusted in this matter to the knowledge which constitutes enlightenment in our age, that there are no answers. So he rests content without general understanding or general meaning. Common sense is enough. He falls back on "experience" and moral stamina, on endurance—a position that has conspicuous elements of nobility, of positive heroism, but that is philosophically uninteresting and, finally, I should think, humanly limited. For common sense has never been enough for the greatest human spirits. A respect for Mr. Frost's work much greater than that of most of the new critics (for I do not insist that poetry be very complex or agree with Mr. Ransom that it should consist of a logical core and a tissue of irrelevancies) makes me hesitant to say so, but it seems to me inescapable that in carrying on Emerson's—to my mind untenable—naturalistic transcendentalism, Mr. Frost has been forced so to hedge and limit and qualify his idealism as to make it finally acceptable neither to Emersonians nor to any variety of moderns.

Mr. Eliot has adopted the Christian myth, with, as I think, considerable increase of power and interest in his poetry. Combining a profound skepticism with a profound faith—and with faith the deeper because of the profundity of the skepticism—combining also arrogance and humility and an incapacity for consistently logical prose and a brilliancy of insight, he has reacted so vehemently from modernism that he has been emotionally impelled to make his reaction complete—in theory at least. But those who conclude that his Christianity necessarily implies his political reaction are mistaken. They ought to be reminded that as he has become more completely a religious poet, many of the attitudes that democratic liberals have found so offensive have become less prominent in the poetry.[4] One might also perhaps recall that a de-

[4] *Notes Toward the Definition of Culture* (New York, 1949) seems to

fensive position calls forth arrogance and superciliousness and extremism; and surely a poet who embraced Christianity in the twenties was in a defensive position. If one wants to search for a "reason" for his anti-democratic attitude, one should look to his early relation with Irving Babbitt and Hulme and Pound, not to his religious opinions. A cause which only occasionally produces a given effect is not a true cause: the late William Temple, Archbishop of Canterbury, and Arnold Toynbee, for example, share the general outlines of Mr. Eliot's religious outlook, but their political views are the opposite of his. At any rate, the fact that Mr. Eliot is more generally considered the major poet of our time than any other poet, and that he has established the canons of both poetry and criticism for the second quarter of the twentieth century, and that he has achieved this position and created this pattern while working within a myth which he has found adequate to his needs—this, it seems to me, should give thoughtful positivists pause. It does not look like simply an accident, though whether the "new failure of nerve" theory of the positivists is a sufficient explanation cannot here be argued. Being neither a philosopher nor a theologian, I can only say that Mr. Eliot's relation to myth

---

me only partially inconsistent with this trend that is so conspicuous in the verse. (And one should not forget what was long ago remarked and is still apparent, the inconsistency between much of Mr. Eliot's prose and his verse.) In *Notes Toward the Definition of Culture,* Mr. Eliot gropes. Many of his admirers must feel that he is not here in command of his subject. Amusingly enough in view of all his warnings against an uncritical attitude toward scientific philosophers, this volume shows him relying in a way that seems to me quite uncritical on one of the least "scientific," in the sense of exact and trustworthy, on one of the most "philosophic" of the sciences, on sociology, and on the work of only one sociologist at that.

seems to me the most crucial factor in his poetry. We may deplore the relationship if we wish. It is a fact toward which we may take an attitude, not a question for debate.

The same thing may be said of the work of Mr. Jeffers. In a manner quite the contrary to that illustrated by Mr. Eliot, Mr. Jeffers has rejected myth as such and tried to maintain a strictly scientific point of view. And this, as I have tried to show, is one of the reasons for the very great weaknesses in his poetry. It is not simply that the particular scientific views to which he holds involve a logical denial of the validity of the poetic experience, of poetry as revelation, and even of man himself; it is that Mr. Jeffers, with what is perhaps the true poet's instinct, has endowed his scientific constructs with concreteness, so that they have become more real for him than the sensible world. One could in fact turn the tables on Mr. Jeffers and argue that he, too, has adopted a myth, that through a naïve use of the fallacy of misplaced concreteness he has dramatized genes and electrons until the total picture he has created, or borrowed, goes as far beyond the known as any religious myth ever has. His myth, however, which he has recently begun to call his "inhumanism," is a particularly barbarous and crude one, philosophically uncritical and logically untenable, the more so perhaps rather than the less because it is based on almost the last word of scientific savants of the fame and caliber of John B. Watson. Rejecting the myths of poetry and religion, he has rejoiced in his subjection to another myth with nothing to recommend it but its supposed status as fact. That no first-rate philosopher of our time, including John Dewey, has ever supposed Mr. Jeffers' myth to be not myth but "facts" is apparently not known, or perhaps not considered important, by Mr. Jeffers. (One of the striking features of our time is that, holding philosophy in contempt, we fall into barbarous philosophies.) What Mr. Jeffers needs even more than better taste and a finer sense of language and a feeling for structure is a valid philosophy. Mr. Jeffers is no Lucretius. A lyric, narrative, and dramatic poet, he has chosen to hold a metaphysic and a myth which confuse and deny him at every point.

Mr. MacLeish, unlike Mr. Jeffers, knows a myth from a lie and from a fact. He seems not to have been able to find a suitable "image of the world." And it is precisely the lack of such an image which helps to weaken "Conquistador" and to limit the meaning and value of many of his other poems. The history of Mr. MacLeish as poet is, like that of Robinson, the history of a man searching for what his world is not ready to supply.

Hart Crane was the most daring of modern American poets. He tried singlehanded to supply the lack which most of the others have felt. If he had succeeded, he would perhaps have been a greater poet than Dante, for Dante did not create the myth he used. (Perhaps, as Mr. Eliot has suggested, no poet ever does, so that Crane could not have succeeded in achieving his ambition no matter how much greater his powers had been than they actually were or how much more suited to his task his temperament.)

In short, most of our poets have not reacted to the influence of science in anything like the simple way predicted by Mr. Richards in the twenties. They have not outlawed knowledge from their poetry as irrelevant to their aims as poets (the poet has learned, Mr. Richards told us in *Science and Poetry,* "that pure knowledge is irrelevant to his aims, that it has no *direct* bearing on

what he should feel, or what he should attempt to do"[5]);
they have not, with the notable exception of Mr. Jeffers,
agreed with Mr. Richards that man "suddenly, not long
ago [*sic*] began to get genuine knowledge on a large
scale";[6] they have not been content to write pure poetry
or to play with attitudes that have no relation to knowledge. (It would seem that whether the creature that looks
like a tarantula really *is* a tarantula or not ["pure knowledge"], has a very direct bearing indeed on what one
should feel and what one should attempt to do.) Despite
the widespread effect of the emotive-referential theory
of language, the final effect of most of the greatest modern
poetry and the great effort of the best modern criticism
have been to show that, in some sense not yet adequately
defined or agreed upon, poetry conveys valid and objective knowledge. Even in their reaction to that "implication" of science which Mr. Richards made his first prem-
ise, the "Neutralization of Nature," the poets have be-
haved in far more complicated ways than Mr. Richards
was led by his confident positivism to expect. Though
they have not all, like Mr. Eliot, defended what Mr. Richards chose to call the "Magical View" of the world ("I
mean, roughly, the belief in a world of Spirits and Powers
.... The belief in Inspiration and the beliefs underlying
Ritual are representative parts of this view"[7]), they have
not, again with the exception of Mr. Jeffers, been content
to accept a view which left knowledge worthless and
values meaningless.

Why they have been so stubborn in their defense of

5 (London, 1926), 57.
6 *Ibid.*
7 *Ibid.*, 52–53.

the meaningfulness and objectivity of value is not clear from a materialist and positivist point of view—unless indeed one agrees with the popular thesis of the twenties expressed by Max Eastman that poets as a class are unusually muddle-headed and that, with the obtuseness characteristic of "the literary mind," they are almost impervious to real knowledge and modern enlightened attitudes. But I imagine few in our day will admit that they agree with the point of view of Mr. Eastman's famous book. I think we must conclude that the reaction of modern American poets to science is not understandable in terms of a philosophy of scientific positivism and materialism.

2. The Defense of Poetry

A study of the relation of the poets to science seems to me to shed some light on the question of the obscurity of much modern poetry. Now the Kenyon reviewers have made it rather clear that only philistines and barbarians are troubled by obscurity in poetry; so that one hesitates to bring up the topic at all for fear of seeming naïve or crass. But there is a problem here for the historian and the critic, a problem that has been for the most part obscured rather than clarified by the writings of most of the new critics. (Mr. Yvor Winters is a notable exception to this generalization; his *Primitivism and Decadence* made a real contribution to an understanding of this problem, whatever one may think of the final validity of his position.) For most of the new critics have been fighting a battle—against the eighteenth and nineteenth centuries, against didacticism, against tradition, sometimes, curiously, fighting tradition in the name of tradition, and against many other things. And what they have been fighting for is the new poetry, the poetry that in English dates from Ezra Pound and T. S. Eliot, especially, as F. R. Leavis has argued, from Mr. Eliot. They have been working out the rationale of a new practice. But they have also been doing more, or their doing this has involved them in something more. They have been defending the importance of poetry in an age of science. The favorite critical question of the twenties, Will poetry survive in a scientific age? was naïve: it carried along with it, as we may see in the early work of Mr. Richards and in such a brash and amusing book as Max Eastman's *The Literary Mind,* too many untenable assumptions. But it was an inevitable question; the typical spokesmen of the age had to ask it. And the new criticism constitutes one-half the answer. The other half is the new poetry itself, which has not only survived but has prospered so greatly that if one were to try to name the most significant events in the literature of the last two decades one might well name more works of poetry than of fiction.

The answer which the new criticism and the new poetry have given to the question asked by the positivists of the twenties goes something like this: Yes, poetry can survive if it has such and such characteristics; and it can survive in this form because this sort of poetry has values which are not the values of science or logic, or philosophy or ethics or practical life, but of the life of the emotions and the imagination, of something for which an old word had to be revived and given a new sense and made into one of the key terms of the new criticism, the *sensibility.*

Now there can be no question that it is science which

has put poetry and criticism of poetry thus on the defensive. Mr. Blackmur has recently argued that urbanization and the decay of tradition are the enemies,[8] but what in the first place created urbanism and made tradition decay? The Southern critics who took their stand on antiscientific agrarianism and general reaction had a clearer notion of what they were fighting against. Critics of the new critics have been very busy of late, but one significant task they have neglected is that of placing modern criticism in a perspective not only of modern culture but of the whole tradition of Western Christendom. Criticizing modern criticism from within the frame of reference of modernism, they have failed to see a number of things.[9] Although there are truths which sympathy alone can reveal, there are also truths which only detachment from the object of study can make clear.

Now if the observational and experimental techniques of science really constitute the only valid approaches to truth, and if the rational humanistic disciplines—sciences, we once dared to call them—are really only meaningless mumbo jumbo, then it follows that poetry, if it is to seem significant, should be pure, should avoid clear, logical statement, should have a logical core only as a thread on which may be hung its tissue of irrelevancies, should be rich in texture and paraphrasable only with difficulty or not at all, should appeal to the sensibility (defined as primarily if not wholly emotional) but not to the

8 "A Burden for Critics," *The Hudson Review*, Vol. I (Summer, 1948), 170–85. Cf. Delmore Schwartz, "The Isolation of Modern Poetry," *Kenyon Review*, Vol. III, No. 2 (Spring, 1941), 209–20.

9 As in Stanley Hyman's evaluation of the Freudian-Marxist-sociological criticism of Kenneth Burke, in *The Armed Vision* (New York, 1948).

reason, should be emotive rather than referential, should include at least seven types of intentional ambiguity, should say whatever it says, if anything, by the interplay of its attitudes and by paradox rather than by statement, should not be didactic, should consist of symbols which must not be allegorical, should be tight, dense, close, complex, rich yet spare, witty, deft, precise, irrelevant, allusive, and ironic. It should have these qualities because only so can it maintain itself in a world in which science monopolizes truth and the rational disciplines are non-sense. It should be thus because only so will it seem to have values which are peculiarly its own rather than pale and inaccurate imitations of scientific truth. It should be thus because in a world in which all values but those of scientific fact have become private, relative, and emo-tional, only thus can it seem to be other than simply a private gratification of the senses, like smoking. It should, indeed it must, be this kind of poetry to be taken seriously: for we cannot take it seriously if it is only poor science (it is clearly very bad science) or if it is concrete and imagi-native and mythic philosophy (philosophy is mumbo jumbo). It must be thus, then, because in a world in which a divorce has been arranged between fact and value, poetry, which cannot compete with science in handling the kind of facts that science handles—and these are thought to be the only *facts* there are—poetry must keep strictly to the realm of value and leave the other realm to science. And it must, as nearly as possible, treat its values as though they were *pure,* denying or minimizing the truth that there are no pure values. Because poetry must be thus, paraphrase is heretical, baroque poetry is necessarily superior to classical poetry, Pound's *Cantos* are a great epic, and James Joyce in *Finnegans Wake* was more poetical than most poets because that work is nothing if not dense, rich, allusive, ironical, witty, symbolic, and, especially, obscure.

Now I do not want to be misunderstood. I am not making a covert attack on the new poetry or the new critics, I do not demand that a poem be easy to paraphrase (though I consider unnecessary obscurity a vice), I am not especially fond of didactic poetry, and I am not married to the nineteenth century. I am making as nearly objective a statement of a reasoned conclusion as I am able. Modern poetry is great, and the new criticism has been of tremendous value, both as the handmaiden of its favorite poetry and as revelation of new insights into the permanent and general nature of poetry. But what is finally clear is that many of the aspects of post-Eliot poetry and the basic strategy of the criticism which has accompanied, rationalized, defended, and promoted it constitute defensive reactions against science, more exactly against a particular set of ideas about science and what it says of the nature of things. This is why obscurity has been openly defended, why complexity has been demanded, why we have been told that the only absolute is the concrete object, why we have been warned to avoid discussion not only of the ideas but even of the emotions in poetry and to limit our attention to the *objects* in it. All this, and much more in the same vein, the most typical critical maneuver of our time, is a neo-nominalist response to a scientific and pseudo-scientific challenge.

Now poetry is different from prose and it always has been; the effort of our time to make it as different as possible is, from one point of view, simply an increased emphasis on those aspects of the nature of poetry which are peculiar to poetry. Poetry is also one of the arts and as an art is different from science; so again the aestheticism of many of the new critics may be viewed as simply an effort to keep distinct things distinct. Poe long ago, having discovered that science was taking all the glamour and mystery from life, invented the heresy of the didactic and limited the rational content of his poems to a minimum on the theory that beauty, not truth, was the sole province of the poem; and no doubt there is more value in Poe's critical theory than Mr. Winters has allowed. But that he was a frightened romantic who was rationalizing his own abilities and incapacities, and that his theory, like the early theory of Mr. Eliot, accounted for and defended his own poetry and certain poems that he liked, but did not even remotely approach justice to the great heritage of Western Christian poetry, should be perfectly clear. Those who do not feel science to be a threat have no need to insist that paraphrasable meaning be minimized in poetry. Coleridge, who even more than Poe is one of the grandfathers of the criticism that has arisen since Mr. Richards, was an immensely greater critic than Poe, but the motivating force behind his speculations was the same as that behind Poe's, the need to justify poetry against science. (The truth of an idea is not to be determined by an analysis of its motivation, but kinship between ideas may thus often be discovered.) From Coleridge to Poe to Mr. Richards is several long steps, but all the steps go in the same direction: in the direction of so narrowing and defining poetry as to take it out of competition with, and thus to make it safe from, science.

Several of these steps, particularly the later ones, need

not have been taken, or taken so precipitately; and one or two of them will some day have to be retraced: not that poetry and science, or poetry and prose, are the same, but that insecurity leads to overcompensation, that defensiveness, though it may permit the avoiding of the danger seen, opens the way to other dangers, and that, finally, poetry does not need to be defended in this way. All this will become clearer as logical positivism and behaviorism, *The Tyranny of Words* and the allure of scientism, *The Meaning of Meaning* and *The Mind in Society* fade farther into the past.

3. *Form and Substance*

One of the most valuable of the many contributions of the new criticism has been its insistence that form and substance are, or ought to be, one. I take it that this idea is as permanently true as any that we are apt to arrive at. But it does not seem to me to necessitate completely omitting the words *meaning* (or *substance* or *content)* and *form* from our discussions of poems. On the contrary, it seems to me that for the purpose of certain valid types of analysis it requires a more intense scrutiny of form to see how it embodies the meaning, and of meaning to see how it both controls and is expressed in the form.

Thus it is clear, for instance, that the form of Robinson's poetry declares his relation to science and the facts of his relation to science throw light on the form of his poetry. The realism of approach and language characteristic especially of his early poems, is certainly connected with the rise of realism and naturalism generally, as it is in the work of Hardy, and so is at least indirectly connected with the influence of science. On the other hand, the involved pseudo-profundity of most of the late long narratives must be thought of in connection with Robinson's philosophy, which was a philosophy of hope without any clear rational basis for hope, and in connection with his religious feeling, which continued to exist without the support or clarification of religious beliefs.

Again, what we need for Mr. Frost's work is not more paraphrase of his easily paraphrasable poems or further studies of the commonness of the common sense in his poems, but close analysis of individual poems and philosophical criticism of the relation of form to idea in the whole body of his work. Mr. Frost is a thoroughgoing conservative: he would conserve even after the reason for conserving is gone. He carries on, as an inheritance which he guards and preserves but cannot increase, a humanistic view of man, which, when it is seen in contrast to modern materialism of the "nothing but" persuasion, is seen to be consonant with and ultimately derived from Christian realism. The historical foundation of his common sense about man is the uncommon sense of Christianity. But in denying the roots, he cuts himself off from further nourishment. Like the lovely useless weed that haunts New England pastures that are going back to woods, the steeplebush, which in a recent volume he has used to symbolize his patient willingness to await the returns of nature's cycles, his work is now an end and only remotely a beginning. Great as it is at its best, it has been no help to younger poets largely because its defense of meaning and value is too personal, its strength too much a matter of temperament. Even technically considered, this is so: for in his respect for "form" Mr. Frost has carried into

211

a new age a taste which is justified neither by the new age—which typically has demanded surrealism, symbolism, and so on, and has produced Joyce and Pound as its typical artists—nor by the old, from which Mr. Frost has cut his ties by his skeptical relativism. Hence in the profoundest sense Mr. Frost's forms are matters of taste and temperament. They are derivative, not in the sense of being borrowed from some other poet, but in the sense of being compounded by temperament out of the traditions of a dead past. Valid traditions continue because the past they carry on is still in some sense alive; but traditions may continue to exist without being really alive. Mr. Frost's poetry is nostalgic for a world which it declares not to exist. Mimesis of form without meaning is an aspect of social and cultural death.

Of Mr. Eliot I have already said so much that I shall say little more here, but I should like to suggest in shorthand form that several of the reasons for his great impact on modern poetry and criticism are related to the problem of form and substance and to the influence of science. For he has united form and substance, used science to describe and denounce a scientific age, and combined a sense of the present with a sense of the vital elements in tradition—so that he neither turns his back on the implications of science nor finds myth unavailable and philosophy contemptible. Hence in his poetry chaos is given shape and the intuition of the poet is given economical and coherent expression. The Christian myth, which cuts him off from so many readers because it seems to them archaic and ridiculous, yet operates to make his obscurity finally meaningful and his impressionism finally objective.

The looseness of form of Mr. Jeffers' poetry is a challenge to critical speculation, for it seems clearly to derive from several sources yet is logically parallel to his philosophy: for in the world which he pictures in his poetry, behaviorism, not *Gestalt,* is the clue to man's place. And if man simply reacts to stimuli as a gasoline engine reacts to the fuel fed into it, if he is not a creative force with power to impose form on things, or if what power he has is deplorable, one should logically expect poetry to aspire to that perfect imitation of subhuman nature which Whitman thought to constitute sufficient form. But though Mr. Jeffers' work is loosely knit, it is not an "imitation of nature" in the only sense in which I can find any meaning in that phrase, that is, automatic writing. But we should, of course, not expect Mr. Jeffers to make his practice perfectly consistent with his theory, for his theory, as we have seen, would lead not only to automatic writing, but on through that to the perfect silence.

If the first fact about the forms adopted by Mr. MacLeish and Hart Crane is that, following the example of Mr. Eliot, they took their cue from the French symbolists, the second is that they found this tradition attractive because it was suited to their age, which more than anything else is the age of science and the machine. If Mr. MacLeish's poems mean anything—if, that is, they are inconsistent with his well-known dictum on the nature of poetry—they mean: here is man's situation, this is the way he is located in time and space. If Hart Crane's poems can be discussed at all, and certainly most of them can be, they must be discussed in terms of ordinary, not ecstatic, logic. And ordinary logic must work out the relations between their forms and the things Crane believed and the ideas he responded to without believing. That his impressionism is related to the modern reluctance to make any explicit interpretation of sensation, a reluctance that may be found equally in Mr. Hemingway's great short stories and in Ezra Pound's to my mind not so great *Cantos,* is clear: the symbolists were discovered, again, because their way was the right way for an age which had discovered that only the simplest values could be relied on to be "real." Crane's obscurest passages are symptoms of that defensive retreat of poetry from science of which I have already spoken, as well as illustrations of the truth that one cannot interpret after the principles of interpretation are destroyed.

4. *Poetry as Document*

If poetry is in some sense an autonomous activity, not properly subordinate to religion or philosophy or politics or practical life, but subject to its own laws and valuable in its own right, yet it is also, like all man's other activities, significant as document for history and philosophy. An intellectual history of the English Renaissance could be written from the works of Shakespeare, Donne, and Milton; and Wordsworth's poems, as Whitehead has shown, imply the whole philosophical problem of the Romantic period. So the larger issues of our time are clearly discernible in the work of our poets, and to talk about the most general significance of modern American poetry is to talk in terms of the history of the recent past. To do so is not to make poetry serve some purpose other than its own, but to acknowledge its importance and uniqueness by including it within the rational effort to understand, which is philosophy.

Modern positivistic naturalism, our poetry says, places us in a dilemma. On the one hand, man is *nothing but* something simpler than, introspectively and intuitively, he seems to be. There has been no emergence; no level of reality is qualitatively unique or irreducible. Man is nothing but an animal, an animal is nothing but a biological mechanism, and biology is finally physics and chemistry. If one replies that there is, after all, *Gestalt* psychology, which finds meaning or something like it irreducible and the whole as much a determinant of the parts as the parts are of the whole; and the new physics, which seems to have shaken the foundations of mechanistic materialism; and social Freudianism, which has modified the biological and materialistic emphases of Freud—if, in short, one alleges that the newer developments in science have shown some tendency to drop the fashion of reductive materialism, then the answer must be made that a fashion three hundred years old is not easily destroyed and that, even after it has been destroyed, its consequences may continue. Strictly contemporary developments in science and philosophy are a different story; they will help to shape a new society, the outlines of which we cannot yet know, and they are already being absorbed by poets, with what ultimate effects we do not know.

But one thing we do know: when John B. Watson, acknowledged leader of American behaviorism, defined man as his physics and chemistry, he was following the lead of three hundred years of science. Although his pronouncements far exceeded the proof and his method turned out to be of limited value, his philosophical generalizations revealed an awareness of assumptions and their implications rare among scientists. He has become the butt of ridicule as an extremist and he has been blamed for giving new arguments to those whose nerve has failed them, but it has yet to be proved that he was not following the time-honored method of science in his attempts to reduce the complex to the simple, to eliminate the mystery, and to explain the fact in terms of its supposed origin or its physical concomitant. In short, his views are extremely significant because they are so perfectly symptomatic of the kind of scientific thought which has shaped our culture and which, more than the newer developments, has influenced the work of the poets we have been considering. If what I am about to quote sounds like a caricature of scientific thinking, I suggest that one consult *The Mind in The Making, The Making of the Modern Mind, The Mind in Society, Why We Behave Like Human Beings,* and similar favorites of the recent past:

The behaviorist began his own formulation of the problem of psychology by sweeping aside all medieval conceptions. He dropped from his scientific vocabulary all subjective terms such as sensation, perception, image, desire, purpose, and even thinking and emotion as they were originally defined. . . . We need nothing to explain behavior but the ordinary laws of physics and chemistry. . . . The behaviorist makes no mystery of thinking. He holds that thinking is behavior, is motor organization, just like tennis, playing golf, or any other form of muscular activity. . . . In one sweeping assumption after another, the behaviorist threw out the concepts both of mind and of consciousness, calling them carryovers from the church dogmas of the Middle Ages. The behaviorists told the introspectionists that consciousness was just a masquerade for the soul.[10]

If man is correctly defined by behaviorism, whether outspoken like that of Dr. Watson or cautiously silent about its philosophy like that of most of the neo-behaviorists, then there should seem logically to be no reason why he should feel lonely in the universe described by physics. But that he has worried about being in an alien universe is clear not only from the work of the poets I have discussed but from the whole course of modern literature. I began my discussion of Robinson by quoting Lord Russell on the concept of the alien universe, and I shall not repeat the quotation, excellent as it is for the comprehensiveness of its statement and the symptomatic tone of its rhetoric. Its point, that value is, alas, unique in man, has often been called the chief revelation of modern science. Only the completely unphilosophical reader was surprised when Joseph Wood Krutch summed up the view as he saw it in his influential lament, *The Modern Temper*.[11]

Now these two deductions from science—that man is nothing but something nonhuman, and that he is in an alien universe—are perfectly inconsistent with each other. Yet they have existed side by side in the same minds. And this suggests something more than that man is capable of believing at the same time two contradictory ideas; it suggests also, and more interestingly, the impos-

[10] John B. Watson, *The Battle of Behaviorism* (London, 1928), 18, 27, 34; and *The Ways of Behaviorism* (New York, 1928), 7.

[11] Influential at least in academic circles. I do not know how much the book influenced the general public. I have examined the thesis of the book in detail in *The South Atlantic Quarterly*, Vol. XXXVII, No. 3 (July, 1938), 282–90. The ideas and attitudes of both Lord Russell and Mr. Krutch were recently re-expressed by W. T. Stace in "Man Against Darkness," *The Atlantic Monthly*, Vol. CXXCII, No. 3 (September, 1948), 53–58, suggesting to me that they are still very much alive.

sibility of finding objective or real value anywhere, inside or outside man, by the methods of post-Renaissance science. In a culture in which the only knowledge supposed to be valid points to these two conclusions, man does indeed find himself in a wasteland. One of the most important things that modern American poetry considered as document says is just that, and not simply the poetry of those poets I have treated, but that of most of the other modern poets, English and American, as well. It is to be read in the poetry of Mr. Auden, who has been immensely influential, and that of Stephen Spender and Day Lewis, or, to choose two from a younger poetic generation, that of Robert Lowell and Dylan Thomas, or to go back several poetic generations, that of Yeats and Hardy. The poetry of our time testifies to both the existence and the importance of what I have called the dilemma of naturalism.

It seems to me likely that the nearly unanimous rejection by the poets of the terms of the dilemma may be explained by reference of the nature of poetry as well as by reference to philosophy. Poets, like businessmen, are impelled to defend their occupation and to see the world in its terms. There is probably an element of rationalization in the poetic defense of value. (But rationalization does not necessarily take us away from the truth; its grounds and processes may be nonlogical and its ends true.) For poetry, like man, and because it involves man's whole humanity, cannot flourish in a waste land. It must find the life-giving water somewhere, somehow. Though there are a few consistent poetic naturalists like Mr. Jeffers—and also I suppose a few Berkeleyan plumbers—the type seems clearly a variation from the norm.

To hold, as many of the new critics have tended to do, that the values which poetry asserts are real for poetry but may not be translated is to depend for defense on a maneuver which cannot ultimately defend. For poetry is but one of man's activities, but part of his total experience, and it must consent to be interpreted, to be document. A poet certainly need not be a philosopher, as Mr. Eliot and his followers have insisted for so long, though there have been, it is well to remember, some great philosophical poets and poems; but the reason is not that didacticism in poetry and paraphrase in criticism are heretical, but that the poet, working as a poet, includes more of total meaning than the scientist or the practical man does, and works more intimately with the concrete wholes that make up the material of total meaning than the philosopher does. Because the latter is true, myth is more common in poetry than abstract philosophy; because the former is true, poetry conveys more humanly relevant, which is to say more meaningful, more philosophical, knowledge about life and man than science does.

We may, then, agree with Mr. Tate when he insists that poetry is neither religion nor social engineering, yet believe that poetry says things, both implicitly and explicitly. It says different things explicitly in different periods, but it says implicitly several things constantly in all periods; so that all modern American poetry implicitly and most of the poets explicitly unite with Dante and Chaucer and Shakespeare in saying with perfect authority that values are real, complex, pervasive; that they are of the essence of our experience; and finally, if I am not mistaken, that they imply the supreme or unifying value which in the past the myth and metaphysic of religion and philosophy have undertaken to define. If these things that poetry says are not in fact true, then we have another problem on our hands in an age already quite over-whelmed by the multiplicity of its problems: the problem of why poets persist in preferring illusion to reality.

And if this is indeed a problem, and if this is the way it ought to be phrased, then we have cause for despair, both critical and philosophical. For this is the problem and the formulation of it of the twenties, and one would have thought that critically and philosophically, if not politically, we had learned in a quarter of a century not to repeat the errors of the hollow men. I think perhaps we have and that the best contemporary criticism has found, and philosophy more modern than modernism will find, that what poetry says is neither simply poetic nor simply illusory but as real as any reality we can possibly discover.

Index

Achievement of T. S. Eliot, The: 69n.
"Aquainted with the Night": 47
Adams, Henry: 143, 182
Adler, A.: 77
Adventures of Ideas: 107n.
Aiken, Conrad: 168
"Alice Doane's Appeal": 18
Alien universe: 8, 18, 21–24, 40–45, 56, 59–60, 81–82, 106–109, 131–32, 198–204, 217–18; growth of concept of, and definition, 6
American Tragedy, An: 61
"American Writer and the New World, The": 152n.
Anthropology: 84–86, 88, 92, 99
Appearance and Reality: 65
Aquinas, St. Thomas: 38
Aristotle: 48
Armed Vision, The: 206n.
"Armful, The": 58–59
Arnold, Matthew: 21
Ash Wednesday: 91
Astronomy: 45, 49, 51, 57, 77, 81, 88, 108–109, 110, 122–24, 127, 141, 143–48, 153, 178, 182–83, 184
"Atlantis": 187–90
Auden, W. H.: *xiii,* 11, 154, 218
Automatic writing: 213
"Ave Maria": 174–75

Babbitt, Irving: 65, 72, 200
Barnett, Lincoln: 134n., 138n.
Barzun, Jacques: 69n.
Battle of Behaviorism, The: 111n., 216, 217n.
"Bear, The": 47
Beard, Charles: 149
Behaviorism: *x*, 12–13, 54, 62, 78–79, 87, 89, 119–20, 113, 144,
     195, 198, 201, 210, 213, 216, 217
Bentley, Arthur F.: 195n.
Bergson, Henri: 55, 62, 65, 66, 67–69, 70, 72, 102
Berkeley, Bishop: 179
Bible, the: 64, 153
Biology: 21, 55, 56, 88, 93, 94, 100, 117, 125, 127, 133, 215
Bishop, John Peale: 133
Blackmur, R. P.: 206
Blake, William: 14
Books That Changed Our Minds: 168n.
Born, M.: 134
Boy's Will, A: 42–43
Bradley, F. H.: 19, 64, 65–67, 72, 114
Bridge, The: 156–92
Bridge of San Luis Rey, The: 189
Bridgman, Percy: 180
Brooks, Cleanth: 17, 74, 83
Bruno, Giordano: 135
"Burden for Critics, A": 206n.
Burke, Kenneth: 206n.
"Burnt Norton": 91
Burroughs, John: 20, 21, 22, 39, 51
Butler, Samuel: 69

Cantos, The: 207, 214
"Cape Hatteras": 157–58, 171, 177, 181, 183, 185, 188, 189
Carman, Bliss: 115

Carnap, R.: 195n.
Carpenter, F. I.: 21n., 25
Catholicism: 39
Cavender's House: 26
Chase, Stuart: 210
Chaucer: 219
Chemistry: 21, 27, 28, 62, 93, 109, 111, 114, 215
Children of the Night, The: 23, 26n.
Christian Science: 39, 168, 169
"Cinema of Man": 136
"Clean, Well-Lighted Place, A": 141
Coleridge, S. T.: 160, 209
"Come In": 48
Conduct of Life, The: 43
"Conquistador": 148–51, 202
Conrad, Joseph: 56, 57
Cowley, Malcolm: 168n.
Crane, Hart: *xiv*, 10, 60, 87, 138n., 155–92, 196, 202, 213–14
Crowther, J. G.: 71n.
"Cutty Sark": 177

"Dance, The": 175, 187
Dante: 87, 163, 166n., 202, 219
"Dark Hills, The": 23
Darwin, Charles: 68, 153
Darwin, Erasmus: 181
Darwin, Marx, Wagner: 69n.
De Broglie, Louis: 134
Decline of the West, The: 170
"Departmental": 58
Descartes: 64
"Desert Places": 48
Determinism: 15, 16, 131; *see also* mechanism
Dewey, John: 4, 37, 63, 64, 79, 195n., 201

Dilemma of naturalism, the: 81, 215–18
Divine Comedy, The: 166n.
Donne, John: 214
Double Axe, The: 130n.
Dreiser, Theodore: 61, 62
Drew, Elizabeth: 86n.
"Dry Salvages, The": 91–99, 173
Du Nouy, Lecomte: *ix,* 34n.

"East Coker": 91
Eastman, Max: 204, 205
Eckhart, Meister: 166
Eddington, Sir Arthur S.: 76, 77, 138n., 139n., 180
Eddy, Mary Baker: 19
Edwards, Jonathan: 113
Einstein, Albert: 45, 51n., 134, 135, 136–40, 143–46, 152,
    171ff., 177ff.
"Einstein": 143–46
Eliot, T. S.: *ix, xii, xiii, xiv,* 10ff., 22, 23, 39, 50, 55n., 58ff.,
    61–104, 112, 113, 131, 133, 135, 140, 141, 143, 149, 150,
    157, 160, 164, 165, 167, 195ff., 199–201, 202, 203, 205,
    208, 209, 212, 213, 219
Emerson, R. W.: *xiii,* 20, 25, 26, 42, 43, 48, 51n., 53, 59, 101,
    102, 162, 164, 166, 176, 199
"Emotions in Words Again": 161n.
Empson, William: 161n.
"End of the World, The": 151
"Epistle to Be Left in the Earth": 146–48, 153
"Eros Turannos": 23
Escape from Freedom: 22
"Essay on Man": 73
"Etherealizing": 50n.
Ethical Studies: 65
Expanding universe: 51, 123–25

Explorations in Personality: 120n.
"Exposed Nest, The": 46

Fallacy of misplaced concreteness: 107–108, 114, 118 ff., 123, 125, 128, 201; defined 66–67
Family Reunion, The: 76, 80, 88
Farrell, James T.: 61
"Fear of God": 50n.
Finnegans Wake: 208
Fire and Ice: 41n., 55n.
Fiske, John: 26
Fitness of the Environment, The: 93
Flagons and Apples: 114
Foerster, Norman: 100
"For the Marriage of Faustus and Helen": 165, 190
Four Quartets: 74, 88, 90, 91, 140, 197; "The Dry Salvages": 91–99
Frank, Waldo: 158n., 166
"Free Man's Worship, A": 23, 81
Freud, Sigmund: 63, 77, 84, 88, 90, 98, 112, 119, 134, 206n., 215
Fromm, Erich: 22, 63
From Ritual to Romance: 85
Frost, Robert: 4, 11, 39, 41–60, 72, 75, 87, 101, 113, 133, 135, 150, 170, 196, 198, 199, 211–12
Functional form: 17, 29–36, 56–58, 82–90, 114–29, 140–51, 171–90, 210–14
Further Range, A: 48

Gardner, Helen: 74, 96
Genetic fallacy ("nothing but"): 6, 8, 9, 27, 28, 78, 79–82, 86–87, 98, 99–100, 103, 107, 109–11, 115–17, 119, 120, 123, 125, 128, 131–32, 198–204, 211, 215–17
Geology: 49, 57, 88, 177, 178, 184
Gestalt psychology: 63, 197, 213, 215

Gledhill, Arthur: 33
God Without Thunder: 155, 193n.
Golden Bough, The: 85
Gulliver's Travels: 150

Hagedorn, Hermann: 20n.
"Hamlet of A. MacLeish, The": 141
"Harbor Dawn": 175
Hardy, Thomas: 210, 218
Hart Crane: 156n,. 158n.
"Hart Crane and the Broken Parabola": 156n.
"Hart Crane's Bridge to Cathay": 156n.
Hawthorne, Nathaniel: 18, 19, 39, 40, 52
Heard, Gerald: 11
"Heart of Darkness, The": 56, 57
Heath, A. E.: 66n.
Heisenberg, W.: 8, 134
Hemingway, Ernest: 44, 57, 140, 146, 154, 214
Henderson, L. J.: 93
Heraclitus: 64, 95, 143
"Hillcrest": 23
History of the Warfare of Science with Theology in Christendom: 20
Hobbes, Thomas: 34n., 133, 134
Hollow Men, The: 61, 62
Hook, Sidney: 79, 100
Horney, Karen: 63
Hulme, T. E.: 65, 69–71, 72, 200
Human Destiny: ix, 34n.
Humanism: 72–73, 99, 100, 139, 211
Hume, David: 179
Huxley, Aldous: 3, 11, 21, 82, 154
"Hyla Brook": 46
Hyman, Stanley: 206n.

Ideas Have Consequences: 107 n.
"Immortal Helix": 137
In Defense of Reason: 63 n., 156 n.
"Indiana": 176, 177
Ingersoll, Robert: 26
"In Hardwood Groves": 43
"Innate Helium": 50 n.
Instrumentalism: 14; *see also* pragmatism
"In the Home Stretch": 46
"Into My Own": 42
Introduction to Metaphysics: 70
"Isaac and Archibald": 23
"Isolation of Modern Poetry, The": 206 n.
"I Will Sing You One O": 46

James, D. G.: 89
James, William: 19, 21, 37, 39
Jeans, Sir James: 76, 77, 81, 108, 109, 134 n., 138 n.
Jeffers, Robinson: 11, 16, 56, 105–32, 141, 143, 144, 150, 201–202, 203, 213, 218
Joyce, James: 208, 212
Jung, C. G.: *ix*, 77, 86 n., 98, 165 n., 166 n.

Kafka, Franz: 62, 126
Kahn, Otto: 156, 157
Kant: 110
Kaplan, Estelle: 20 n.
Kenyon Review: 74, 204
Kierkegaard, S.: 62
King Jasper: 23, 27
Knowing and the Known: 195 n.
Krishna: 64, 96
Krutch, J. W.: 21, 79, 127 n., 217

Laforgue, J.: 86 ff., 94

Laforguian irony and the genetic fallacy: 86–88, 94
"Land's End": 139
Langer, Susanne K.: 18, 30n., 37, 89
Language and Reality: x, 15, 30n., 89n., 105, 162n., 197
Leavis, F. R.: 205
Lewis, C. Day: 218
Light of Day, The: 21
"Lines for a Prologue": 136
Link, Henry C.: 4, 62
Literary Mind, The: 204, 205
"Literature as Knowledge": 195n.
"Little Gidding": 92
Logical positivism: 29, 49, 66, 89, 193–94, 195, 210
London, Jack: 126
"Love Song of J. Alfred Prufrock, The": 13, 79, 82
Lowell, Robert: 218
Lucretius: 84, 133, 202

MacLeish, Archibald: 21, 87, 133–54, 181, 196, 202, 213
Making of the Modern Mind, The: 216
"Man Against Darkness": 217n.
"Man Against the Sky, The": 22, 29–36
Mann, Thomas: 34n.
"Margrave": 121–29
Marxism: *ix, xii*, 4, 102, 206n.
Masque of Mercy, A: 42
Masque of Reason, A: 45, 50n., 53, 54
Materialism: *viii*, 27, 32, 54, 61ff., 68, 70, 72–73, 78, 101, 102,
    133, 153, 198, 204, 211, 215; defined, 3–17, esp. 7; *see also*
    mechanism *and* naturalism
Matthiessen, F. O.: 65, 69
Meaning of Meaning, The: 89, 195, 197, 210
Mechanism: 27ff., 32, 69, 153, 215; *see also* materialism *and*
    naturalism

Melville, Herman: 160
Mencken, H. L.: *ix*, 62
Metaphor: 196–97
Milton, John: 214
Mind in Society, The: 210, 216
Mind in the Making, The: 216
"Miniver Cheevy": 23, 37
Minkowski, Herman: 138n.
"Modern Poetry": 158, 162, 165
Modern Poetry and the Tradition: 83n.
Modern Temper, The: 21, 127n., 150, 217
Morgan, George Jr.: 6n.
"Morning at the Window": 97
Morris, Charles W.: 195n.
Morris, Lloyd: 20n.
Mountain Interval: 46
Murder in the Cathedral: 80, 88
Murphy, Gardner: 120n.
Murray, Henry A.: 120n.
"My November Guest": 43
Mysterious Universe, The: 109n., 134n.
Mysticism and Logic: 24n.
Myth: *ix, x,* 16, 42, 85, 159, 167, 172, 176, 190, 191, 193–94, 198ff., 212, 219; defined, 193

Naturalism: *ix,* 7ff., 19ff., 23, 24, 28, 56, 59, 61ff., 73, 100, 199, 215; materialistic naturalism defined, 7; *see also* mechanism *and* materialism; *for* organic naturalism, *see* Whitehead
"Nature" (Emerson): 42
Nature and Destiny of Man, The: 41, 152n., 193
Nature and Life: 180n.
Nature of Literature, The: 197n.
"Need of Being Versed in Country Things, The": 47

"Nevertheless One Debt": 152 n.
New Criticism, The: 89 n.
"New England": 23
New Hampshire: 46
New Introductory Lectures on Psychoanalysis: 112 n.
New Pathways in Science: 139 n.
Newton, Isaac: 138, 139, 174, 181
Niebuhr, Reinhold: 3, 41, 62, 152 n., 193
Nietzsche, Friedrich: 19, 20, 37, 105, 115, 126, 129, 133
Nominalism: 107, 194, 208
North of Boston: 46
"Notes on Obscurity": 133
Notes Toward the Definition of Culture: 199 n., 200 n.
"Nothing Gold Can Stay": 47
"Now Close the Windows": 43

Objective correlative, the: 88–90
Obscurity in relation to science: 204–10
"Once by the Pacific": 47
On the Limits of Poetry: 89 n., 195 n.
Open World, The: 34 n.
Ouspensky, P. D.: 161, 162 n., 164, 166, 167, 169, 171, 181,
    186 ff., 190
"Out, Out —": 46
"Oven Bird, The": 46

Pareto, Vilfredo: 210
"Passage to India": 155, 157, 190
"Peaceful Shepherd, The": 47
Personality: A Biosocial Approach to Origins and Structure:
    120 n.
Philosophy in a New Key: 18, 37 n., 89 n.
Philosophy in the Poetry of E. A. Robinson: 20 n.
Physics: x, 5, 6, 8 ff., 21, 31, 32, 34 n., 38, 52, 56, 66, 67, 69, 70,

93, 109, 111, 134, 136 ff., 139 n., 143–46, 153, 169, 177, 179 ff., 192, 198, 215
Planck, M.: 8, 134
Plato: 41, 43, 48, 50, 137
Poe, E. A.: 77, 160, 209
Poems, 1924–1933 (MacLeish): 141
Poetry of E. A. Robinson, The: 20 n.
Pollock, T. C.: 89, 197
Popular Science Monthly: 7 n., 20
Positivism: *viii*, 28, 38, 49, 78, 102, 194, 195 n., 196 ff., 204, 205, 215; defined, 7
Pound, Ezra: 69, 71, 87, 160, 200, 205, 207, 212, 214
Powell, L. C.: 116 n.
Pragmatism: 4, 52, 53; *see also* instrumentalism
"Preludes": 80
Primitivism and Decadence: 83 n., 156 n., 204
Principles of Literary Criticism: 160, 195
Principles of Logic: 65
Protestant modernism: 26, 54, 71
Psychological Types: 166 n.
Psychology (and psychoanalysis): 22, 28, 51, 69, 79, 80, 88 ff., 98, 100, 103, 109, 110, 112, 119, 133, 134, 165 n., 197, 216
Psychology and Religion: 166 n.
Pure poetry: *vii, viii*, 196–97, 205–207

"Quaker Hill": 185, 188
Quantum theory: 138 n., 139 n., 180

Rajan, B.: 63 n.
Ransom, J. C.: 89, 155, 193, 199
Reflections on Violence: 71
Relativism: 15, 90
Relativity, theory of: 134, 135, 136–40, 153, 169, 171 ff., 177 ff.
"Reluctance": 43

"Reproach to Dead Poets": 140
Richards, I. A.: *vii, viii, ix*, 89, 90, 106, 160, 161, 162 n., 164, 165, 194, 195, 202–204, 205, 209
Richards, Laura: 33
"Riders": 53
Rimbaud, Arthur: 87, 160
"River, The": 175
Roan Stallion: 109
Robinson, E. A.: *xiv*, 4, 10, 18–40, 41, 43, 57 ff., 72, 75, 87, 102, 131, 133, 136, 142, 195–96, 198, 202, 210–11, 217
Robinson Jeffers: The Man and His Work: 116 n.
Rock, The: 55 n., 67, 76, 88
Rousseau, J. J.: 72
Royce, Josiah: 19, 21, 37
Russell, Bertrand: 23, 30, 39, 60, 67, 76, 81, 132, 217

Sacred Wood, The: 13
"Sand Dunes": 52
Santayana, George: 19, 20, 21
Scepticism and Poetry: 89 n.
Schopenhauer, Arthur: 19, 20, 37
Schrödinger, E.: 134
Schwartz, Delmore: 206 n.
Science and Health: 19
Science and Poetry: vii, 89, 195, 202
Science and the Modern World: 38, 61, 168
Science for a New World: 66 n.
Scientific humanism: 33
Scientific Outlook, The: 67 n.
Scientism: 9, 52, 67–68, 72–75, 84, 210; defined, 6–8
"Seafarer": 136
"Second Thoughts About Humanism": 99–100
Secularism: 62, 102
Selected Letters of E. A. Robinson: 20 n.

"Selene Afterwards": 139
Semantics: *vii,* 4, 5, 12, 50, 63, 89, 102, 194–95, 203
Semiotic: 194–95
Sensibility: 11–13, 17, 143, 205; defined, *xi;* dissociation of,
    18–19, 22–23, 35–40, 44–45
Shakespeare: 87, 125, 138, 214, 219
Shapley, Harlow: 7, 8
Shaw, Bernard: 76
"Signature for Tempo": 140
"Significance of 'The Bridge,' The": 156 n.
"Sitting by a Bush": 53
"Skeptic": 50 n.
Smith, Bernard: 168 n.
Social Relations of Science, The: 71 n.
Sociology: 8, 22, 84, 200 n., 206 n.
"Sonnet—To Science": 77
Sorel, G.: 71
Southern critics, the: 206
Speculations: 69, 70
Spencer, Herbert: 19, 20, 37, 39, 134
Spender, Stephen: 11, 218
Spengler, Oswald: *ix,* 62, 129, 167, 170, 176, 187
Spinoza: 135
Stace, W. T.: 217 n.
"Star Splitter, The": 46
Steeple Bush: 48
Stevens, Wallace: *xiii,* 64, 196
"Storm Fear": 43
Stovall, Floyd: 21 n.
Study of History, A: 61
Surrealism: 212
Sutcliffe, Denham: 20 n.
Swift, Jonathan: 150
Symbolism: 83, 87, 88, 105, 142, 160, 212 ff.

Tate, Allen: 31 n., 89, 195 n., 196, 219
Temple, William: 200
Tennyson, Alfred: 21, 136
Tertium Organum: 161 n., 169
Theology: 20, 25, 26, 33, 34, 38, 50, 71, 85, 88, 135, 152, 174
Thermodynamics, second law of: 54–55, 69, 108 n., 147 n.
Thomas, Dylan: 218
Thomism: 62
Thompson, Lawrence: 41 n., 53, 55
Thoreau, H. D.: 52, 60
Thoughts After Lambeth: 76
"Three Songs": 185
Thursoe's Landing: 116
"To Aileen-of-the-Woods": 114
"To Brooklyn Bridge": 171
Toynbee, Arnold: *ix,* 61, 62, 85, 94, 200
T. S. Eliot: The Design of His Poetry: 86 n.
"The Tunnel": 185, 187, 188
Twain, Mark: 134
Tyndall, John: 8
Tyranny of Words, The: 50, 210

Uncertainty principle (Heisenberg's principle of indeter-
    minancy): 9, 180
Universe and Dr. Einstein, The: 134 n., 138 n.
Untriangulated Stars (letters of E. A. Robinson): 20 n.
Urban, W. M.: *x,* 15, 16, 30 n., 89, 105, 162 n., 197
"Uriel": 51 n., 53

"Vantage Point": 43
"Van Winkle": 175
"Verses for a Centennial": 138
Voltaire: 84
"Voyages II": 192

Waste Land, The: 62, 74, 83 ff., 88, 99, 150, 160

Watson, John B.: 28, 54, 62, 78, 87, 101, 110, 111, 119, 201, 215, 217

Wave mechanics: 138 n., 139 n.

Ways of Behaviorism, The: 216, 217 n.

Weaver, Richard: 107 n.

Weber, Brom: 156, 158 n., 160 n., 165 n., 170 n., 174, 175, 188

Wells, H. G.: 76

"West-Running Brook": 47, 54, 55

Weyl, H.: 8, 34 n., 138 n.

Wheelwright, Philip: 63

White, A. D.: 20

Whitehead, Alfred North: x, 8, 28, 38, 61, 62, 66, 76, 107 n., 114, 117, 135, 167, 168, 171, 180, 214

Whitman, Walt: 20, 157–59, 161 ff., 167, 171, 175 ff., 182 ff., 188, 189, 192, 213

Why We Behave Like Human Beings: 216

Wilde, Oscar: 160

Wilder, Thornton: 189

"Wild Grapes": 47

Williams, Charles: *ix*

Williams, W. C.: 196

"Winter Eden, A": 47

Winters, Yvor: 30 n., 36 n., 63, 64, 83, 155, 156 n., 159, 170, 204, 209

Witness Tree, A: 48

Wordsworth, William: 14, 214

World's Body, The: 89 n.

Wright Brothers, the: 183

Yeats, W. B.: 4, 141, 218

"You, Andrew Marvell": 143, 144, 151

Zola, Emile: 16, 61

F